EMILY CARTER

SELF-REGULATION
WORKBOOK
for Teens

Coping Skills and CBT Exercises
for Teens to Improve Self-Control,
Master Emotions, Resist Impulsive
Behavior, and Uplift Yourself
When Feeling Down

TABLE OF CONTENTS

Your Free Gift V

Introduction 1

PART 1: CBT COGNITIVE TECHNIQUES

Chapter 1: Introduction to Cognitive Behavioral Therapy (CBT)   4

     Exercise 1: Goal-Setting 9

Chapter 2: Understanding Thoughts, Feelings, and Behaviors   12

Chapter 3: Challenging Negative Thinking Patterns   17

     Exercise 2: Reframing Negative Thoughts. 20

     Exercise 3: Creating Balanced Thoughts. 23

Chapter 4: Building Positive Self-Talk   26

     Exercise 4: Practicing Positive Self-Talk 28

     Exercise 5: Challenge the Negative Self-Talk 33

     Exercise 6: Affirmations. 36

     Exercise 7: Positive Coping Statements. 39

Chapter 5: Mindfulness and Acceptance   42

     Exercise 8: Five Senses Mindfulness 45

     Exercise 9: Body Scan Meditation 46

     Exercise 10: Box Breathing 47

     Exercise 11: Mindful Walking 48

     Exercise 12: Acceptance Practice. 49

     Exercise 13: Gratitude Practice 55

PART 2: CBT BEHAVIORAL TECHNIQUES

Chapter 6: Understanding Behavior Patterns   64

    Exercise 14: The ABC Model in Use. 66

    Exercise 15: Common Triggers 76

Chapter 7: Developing Coping Skills   80

Chapter 8: Behavioral Activation   85

    Exercise 16: Mood and Activity Diary. 87

    Exercise 17: SMART Goal-Setting. 90

    Exercise 18: Behavioral Activation Worksheet 99

    Exercise 19: Activity Experiment 101

    Exercise 20: Positive Activity Catalog 104

Chapter 9: Assertiveness Training   109

    Exercise 21: Assertive Communication Role-Play 112

    Exercise 22: Assertive Communication Scenarios 113

Chapter 10: Problem-Solving Skills   116

    Exercise 23: Problem-Solving Steps Practice 120

    Exercise 24: Solving Common Problems 126

    Exercise 25: Solution Implementation Practice. 141

Chapter 11: Relapse Prevention   143

Conclusion 148

Thank You 150

About The Author. 151

References 152

YOUR FREE GIFT

To really make the most out of your life, and to succeed in it, it's crucial to never stop learning. To further develop your knowledge of important life skills, I've got something for you... something you can really be excited about!

As a way of saying thank you for your purchase, I want to offer you some BONUSES completely FREE of charge:

To get instant access, just go to:

https://lifeskillbooks.com

Here's just a glimpse of what is included:

BONUS 1

Unleashing Your Potential: A Teenager's Guide to Developing a Growth Mindset and Opening Your Path to Success

Inside the book, you will discover...

- ✧ The differences between a fixed and growth mindset, how your mindset impacts your personal growth and success, and why a growth mindset is the one you should adopt.

- ✧ Practical strategies to cultivate a growth mindset, from daily habits to overcoming obstacles.

- ✧ How to utilize a growth mindset to supercharge your academic and career success.

- ✧ And much more!

BONUS 2

The Anxiety Handbook: Understand the Types, Triggers and Symptoms of Anxiety to Effectively Cope With It

Inside this comprehensive guide, you will discover...

✧ Insights into different types of anxiety disorders, so you can understand and identify specific triggers.

✧ Overview of the symptoms of each anxiety type so you can learn to recognize them better.

✧ Proven techniques to manage and reduce anxiety, helping you regain control over your life.

✧ And more!

BONUS 3

Printable Self-Regulation & Coping Skills Worksheets: Practical Tools for Managing Stress, Anxiety and Emotions

Inside this comprehensive workbook, you will discover...

✧ **Step-by-Step Coping Strategies**: Gain access to structured exercises that help you identify, challenge, and reframe negative thoughts, leading to a more positive mindset.

✧ **Personalized Mood and Habit Tracking**: Utilize detailed trackers to monitor your mood and daily habits, allowing you to identify patterns and make informed changes for better mental health.

✧ **Self-Care and Mindfulness Practices**: Engage in a 30-day self-care challenge and explore various self-soothing techniques to promote relaxation and reduce stress.

✧ **Interactive and Easy-to-Use Worksheets**: Enjoy a user-friendly layout with guided prompts and questions designed to support your journey toward improved mental well-being and personal growth.

✧ **And more!** Everything is in easily printable form.

Now, go to the website below for instant access to these and several other amazing bonuses. Completely free of charge.

https://lifeskillbooks.com

INTRODUCTION

"Rule your mind or it will rule you."– Horace

Sounds like a pretty powerful saying, doesn't it? But it seems like lately, all you ever do is let go. You let go of the things that surround you; you let go of every aspect of you; you let go of your thoughts and let them wander around. You notice they're reaching places you don't really want to go, but you go there anyway.

But you've been doing this for a while. In the beginning, it didn't seem like such a scary thing to indulge in. Now, it looks like you've completely changed yourself. When you look in the mirror, you are unrecognizable – and not just physically, but emotionally and mentally too. What happened? When did you decide to hand over control over yourself completely to your mind? In retrospect, was it a good idea?

Go back to the saying, "Rule your mind, or it will rule you." Think about this for a moment. Is it really a good idea to hand everything over to your mind? I mean, it is your most powerful tool, so why not give full control to it?

But you already know the answer to this question. Do you know how I know that? Because you already gave full permission to your mind, and you noticed that it led you astray. It started going to the deepest and darkest corners, ultimately dragging you along. And you were never able to escape from its claws. You succumbed to its power, and now you feel helpless. You are stuck in a vortex of unpredictable behavior and negative thoughts. Of course, you want to step away from that – who wouldn't?

I welcome you to the beginning of the most magnificent and transformative journey you will ever walk on. There is only one project in life you will constantly need to work on – and that is yourself. I am assuming you picked up this book because somewhere deep inside you, you noticed that a change should happen. You notice how incredible you can be and that something is holding you back. That something is yourself and yourself only.

My name is Emily, and I am so glad you allowed me to be a part of your transformative journey. Over the course of these pages, I will try to transfer some of my passion for helping others to you. I have taken most of the examples, exercises, and basically everything in this book from my personal experience. Noticing that there was a gap in my life skills later in life made me realize that I had missed out on plenty. So, while I managed to learn everything I wanted and came out on the other side swinging, I still wanted to help others.

That's how this book came to be. Without giving it much thought, I sat down and started writing. I implemented everything I did and created such a bullet-proof plan that you are hardly ever challenged to make a mistake. What helped me the most during my personal journey was the Cognitive Behavioral Therapy (CBT) approach – which is the book's main topic.

Together, we will explore the CBT method, how it can help you, and how it can be the pillar upon which you will build your self-regulation goals. Whenever you felt like you needed help understanding your thoughts, feelings, and behavior, there was no one to help you – until now! Together, we will cover so much – how to identify and challenge your negative thinking patterns, how to tap within yourself and create balanced and realistic thoughts, and how to focus on building yourself up through the power of positive self-talk.

On top of that, I even touch upon the most well-known CBT behavioral techniques. As you turn the pages, you will discover them, and the best thing about them is that you can try them on your own! How so? I have meticulously added exercises in almost every chapter. While these are small, their impact will be of great benefit to you. They will help you understand better what is written on these pages and help you to understand yourself better. This book is all about being assertive, being smart, developing the best coping skills, and understanding the core of who you are. It is about learning, constantly developing, and working on yourself. For without work, there is no change.

Last but not least, I dedicate the last chapter to you for all of you who are still doubting that this book has the power to change your life. It is all about preventing yourself from entering that swirl of negativity you're so desperately trying to get out of. It is the cherry on top of everything you will learn while reading this book!

I truly hope that what you find between these pages will empower you to develop and grow into the best and brightest version of yourself!

So don't wait any longer – turn the page and allow me to help you reinvent yourself!

PART

01

CBT COGNITIVE TECHNIQUES

CHAPTER

INTRODUCTION TO COGNITIVE BEHAVIORAL THERAPY (CBT)

"You have the power over your mind – not outside events. Realize this, and you will find strength." – Marcus Aurelius

Well, you're here, at the beginning of your journey, desperately trying to control everything around you – and yourself. If you have picked this book up, it probably means that you truly are struggling to find your way in this chaotic world.

I am here to tell you that it is okay – it is okay to feel what you're feeling. It is okay to think what you're thinking, and it is even okay to be surprised by everything new that comes your way. Whether you are dealing with some kind of an emotional issue, or you have noticed a behavioral pattern within you that you'd like to change, or maybe even some self-limited thinking, this book can be the answer to everything you're searching for.

In this chapter, together, we are going to start our journey filled with wisdom, and deep insight, and open the magical doors of cognitive behavioral therapy. Here, you will have the ultimate chance to get to know yourself and become a better version of you. Allow me to introduce CBT through a few subchapters.

The Principles of Cognitive Behavioral Therapy

Let's start from the very beginning. Do you know what cognitive behavioral therapy means? CBT is a skill-based psychotherapy treatment that can help people get in control of their feelings, thoughts, and emotions, so they can navigate through life easily. This approach can help you spot the negative influences on your mind and soul and the patterns that result in more harm than good. As a concept, CBT is time-based, goal-orientated, and a very well-

4

structured treatment. Whether you are dealing with depression, anxiety, or any other type of disorder, this approach can help you subsequently change your view of yourself and the world.

By reframing your thoughts, you can improve your overall quality of life. So far, things sound appealing, don't they? Let's explain further. To get into the CBT scheme, you need to know the basic principles. These are considered to be more of "levels" rather than principles. Here they are:

1. **Your core beliefs** – you start from the very beginning – who are you? How do you view yourself? What do you believe in? Do you know that the core beliefs represent the strongest childhood experiences? If you look within yourself, you can discover a whole world filled with beliefs about your future, yourself, your environment, and so on. These beliefs are deeply rooted, and it is your task to uncover them.

2. **Wrong assumptions** – these types of assumptions can be very discouraging about your entire well-being. You are young, filled with energy and hope – but what you're probably not aware of is that people generally hold on to the bad rather than the good. This type of action is classified as a cognitive distortion. Imagine having a lot of irrational thought patterns – seems like, over time, they might take over your perception of reality, right?

3. **A negative way of thinking** – which ultimately leads to overall negative perceptions of reality. After a while of succumbing to the negative patterns and thoughts, they will become your reality. You will start noticing that they have become a habit. The tricky part about them is that they are very short, and they can stir up negative emotions, making them difficult to recognize. However, don't mistake these automatic negative thoughts with the "common" negative thoughts. All of us are human beings after all, and it is only natural to have distorted thoughts* every once in a while. But, when this turns into a habit, that's when you should become alert.

*Distorted thoughts are also known as cognitive distortions. When this happens, you usually believe that one mistake defines your entire being and that the particular mistake makes you a failure. That leads to the belief that you should try to never make mistakes again. Finally, it all results in overgeneralization – thinking that you can never get something right and that things will never get better.

CBT can help you realize that you don't always have to believe in what you think. It will also help you realize that every time you are faced with a challenge, a difficult emotion, or a distortive thought, you have a choice. You can always be kinder, starting by sharing kindness with yourself, and then everything around you.

How CBT Can Benefit Teens

Let's put things into perspective here, shall we? I challenge you to a little thinking game – called action and reaction. You have probably noticed the ever-so-slight changes that happen when you have positive or negative thoughts. What changes did you notice happening (physically) whenever a distorted thought goes through your mind? In contrast, what kind of change do you notice happening when a positive thought overwhelms your mind?

Emotions affect behavior – that is something almost every teen is blissfully unaware of. Your thoughts, emotions, and behaviors are all linked. The first one is the thought – usually caused by a certain situation. The thought is your interpretation of an event. Then comes the emotion. The emotion is the second one in line, and it is triggered by what you thought of earlier on. In most cases, especially with teens, this emotion turns to the negative side. Finally, the behavior enters the scene. The negative emotions you feel influence your behavior, leading to you acting in a way you might regret later.

So, how can CBT help you prevent this negative vortex from further developing into a part of your personality?

CBT is known to have both short and long-term benefits. First, we tap into the short-term ones:

✧ This type of therapy shows fast results. Many psychologists and therapists use it to help young people overcome challenges in life. The average time it takes to get deeply familiarized with the CBT skillset is about 15 sessions. The alternative to that is reading carefully selected material with exercises that help you achieve your goal - this book!

✧ The activities you may encounter are engaging – meaning you won't have to sit and listen all the time, but rather take matters into your own hands. You get involved, and through a very interesting concept, you change yourself.

✧ You are held accountable for your own actions – but don't let this fool you, this is not a negative concept. You are empowered to take control of your life. You constantly apply the new principles you learn.

Together, we slowly approach the long-term benefits of CBT for teens. After a while of working on yourself, you will discover that this is an effective way to increase self-awareness and emotional intelligence – which is ultimately the path to living a healthy and happy life. As time passes, you will notice the following long-term benefits:

✧ You will start to respond to stress in a healthier way. Whenever you are faced with a negative thought or a challenging situation, you shift them toward a realistic or positive attitude and approach them the same way. Not letting anxiety, fears, and phobias take over is an excellent step forward.

✧ Being more compassionate – for some of you, this seems like a state you might never be able to achieve. Well, you couldn't be more wrong about that! You will find that compassion is within you, around you, and a constant part of your life.

✧ Reduce the unhealthy behavior you've indulged in for so long. The negative thoughts you had about yourself, the interactions with other people – all the situations in your life will become something you manage with skill and grace rather than tension and negativity.

With these goals in mind, it is time to look within – and learn the concept of self-regulation.

Setting Goals for Self-Regulation

Being a distressed teen can't be easy – you are constantly thinking that you live in a world where you don't belong anywhere, you allow these negative thoughts to overwhelm your mind, and it seems like you're failing each challenge you face. Keeping the weight of the world on your shoulders is not an easy job to do – and it is also not your job to do too. The sooner you realize that the easier it will be for you to move on and step into a more centered and powerful version of yourself.

What is self-regulation? It is a skill that many teens struggle to obtain at first – mostly because emotions play a big role in their lives. However, self-regulation means being able to manage your thoughts, your emotions, and your behavior, no matter what surrounds you. Having self-regulating skills can help you pull away from the emotional disturbance you've been experiencing, and it can help you navigate the tasks, challenges, and responsibilities more easily.

All of this seems good in theory, but when it comes to practice, how can you implement it?

Now, before you plunge head-first into making some severe changes in your life, you need to understand what kind of difference you want to achieve. Once you've determined who you are, where you are, and where you want to go, you can start utilizing the techniques and skills to complete your goal.

When you clearly know your starting point, setting up some goals can help you outline the path you want to walk to get there. The goals you will start developing will help you achieve the self-regulation act. For example, you can set a goal to react calmly in challenging situations – for instance, you can set a goal that your initial reaction to someone declining your invitation for a cup of coffee would be calm, centered, and respective of the others.

The process of setting goals will not be complete without your willpower, perseverance, and the understanding that those people who have managed to achieve this calm, is because they have made self-regulation their "default setting." Have you ever encountered someone so calm – be that a professor, your parent, or anyone else from your environment, that their calmness made you aware of yourself and your own behavior? Depending on one teen to the next, that kind of calm behavior can either lead to a reaction where you're embarrassed about your way of acting or it may make you want to act out. Needless to say, both situations are far from ideal.

Setting goals is a part of being proactive – and realizing that you want to possess that calmness that you have witnessed in others. You want to be powerful; you want to be in control, and you want to know how to handle yourself in every situation. With this in mind, how do you actually start setting goals? That's where I come into the picture to help.

If you could skip ahead in time where you've obtained all the knowledge and skills necessary to master self-regulation. How would your life be different from the one you're living today? Would anything change? If yes, what? Which are the first specific things that came into your mind – something that changed for the better? Are there some things you can do better than today?

Read through the first exercise below. See what you need to do and start working!

GOAL-SETTING

In this exercise, you are going to set some goals that will allow you to start working on fully stepping into your power.

First step – write down your ultimate goals. While you are writing down your goal, make it well-defined. For example, you can write down "Become more in charge of my emotions." Consider these goals to be the changes you want to see happening to you.

Second step – add a description of each goal, and what it would mean to you to achieve it. Think of this as breaking down your goals into more specific pieces. Use a detailed description to get rid of a certain issue you've been dealing with or use that detailed description to describe your future self. As an addition to the previous example, you can be more specific about it, by saying something like, "Becoming more in charge of my emotions will mean dedicating more time to myself, learning how to be more centered, calm, etc".

Third step – start thinking about the actions you need to take to achieve these goals. These actions need to help you remain consistent and on the right track – something that can show you you're getting closer to reaching your goals. To continue with the same example, you can do the following - "Meditate each day, keep a gratitude journal, channel your energy to positive things, indulge in mindfulness exercises, etc." By making your goal specific you are actually creating a bullet-proof action plan.

Ultimately, each of your goal-setting points should look similar to the example below:

<u>The ultimate goal</u>: Become more in charge of my emotions.

<u>The specific goal</u>: Becoming more in charge of my emotions will mean dedicating more time to myself, learning how to be more centered, calm, etc.

<u>Actions I take to make it happen</u>: Meditate each day, keep a gratitude journal, channel my energy to positive things, indulge in mindfulness exercises, etc.

Now, go ahead and write down at least five goals of yours following the steps above:

_____

_____

_____

_____

_____

_____

_____

_____

_____

_____

_____

_____

_____

By doing this exercise you will be able to tap deep within yourself and uncover the core of your being – and that is the first step toward improvement.

Cognitive behavioral therapy can be fun – as long as there is someone like me who can guide you through the process, break everything down into smaller pieces, and show you that, as long as you keep putting one foot in front of the other (no matter the pace) you can get to your ultimate goal of being better.

What Did You Learn From This Chapter?

As a first chapter, it seemed pretty exciting, right? To sum up, here is what you learned from it:

- ✧ What is cognitive behavioral therapy.
- ✧ What are the three principles of CBT.
- ✧ Distorted thoughts and how they affect your quality of life.
- ✧ Thoughts, emotions, and behaviors are connected – they represent the cycle you are most likely trying to step out of.
- ✧ There are both long-term and short-term benefits of applying CBT in your life.
- ✧ Self-regulation – what it is and how you can use it to improve yourself.
- ✧ How to set goals for self-regulation.

Cognitive behavioral therapy is the key to creating a stronger and more powerful version of yourself. Now, over the course of this book, I will keep focusing on explaining every little detail that you might think we've overlooked. For example, take a look at what the next chapter is about! We discuss what I mentioned earlier – the process of thought, emotion, and behavior – how it affects your life and how it shapes you into an individual. Turn the page and discover all you need to know about it!

CHAPTER 02

UNDERSTANDING THOUGHTS, FEELINGS, AND BEHAVIORS

"The happiness of your life depends upon the quality of your thoughts." –
Marcus Aurelius

Before we continue any further, I need you to realize one thing – no person is immune to life's challenges. No matter what has happened to you and how you experienced certain situations, this is something that will always leave an impact and slightly alter you. After every event that occurs, be that a positive or a negative one, the remains of the experience are what your mind deems important, and that's what's left – long after the event has finished.

But, to truly tap within yourself and uncover "what you're made of," you need to know how to do that first. As a most likely inexperienced young mind, you don't really know where to begin. While in the first chapter, we recognized the essential dots that need connecting, in this chapter, I am helping you delve deep within yourself, dissecting the very core of who you are.

The concepts we will cover together here will help you better understand your thoughts, feelings, and behaviors as well as how to manage them.

Identifying Automatic Thoughts

From the moment you wake up to the moment you fall back asleep, thousands of thoughts pass through your mind. Some are wonderful and happy and fill you with joy, while others are negative and make you feel bad. There are many reasons why this happens, especially when it comes to automatic negative thoughts.

Overall, automatic thoughts are what we think of instantly – kind of as a first response to anything that happens around us or to us. These thoughts are mostly triggered by an outside source, but how you manage them in your mind and what you connect them with is what matters. Let's talk about automatic negative thoughts.

These automatic negative thoughts happen for various reasons. For example, teens who are dealing with anxiety or mood swings are more prone to experience negative thinking. Now, don't get me wrong – the automatic negative thoughts are sometimes what helps us survive, but if this is your constant state of mind, then you need to change something. It is a way of "anticipating threats" in a way.

These automatic thoughts connected to a negative thinking pattern are usually a result of your core beliefs and previous experiences. So, your automatic thoughts are actually what you truly believe about yourself, your future, and the world around you.

With that in mind, it is time to start identifying the automatic thoughts (especially the negative ones). Most of the time, people have a difficult time doing this at first, and if that happens to you, remember that it's okay. That is why CBT can help you open doors of your mind you haven't even been aware of until now.

There is a key to identifying automatic thoughts: looking for what first comes to mind when an emotion arises. For example, you open your Instagram account, and you see that your friends got together for a cup of coffee but didn't invite you. How would that make you feel? The immediate response you have is your automatic thought. It can be positive – where you think, "Oh good, it's such a nice day, I hope they're having a good time," or negative – "They didn't invite me, I'm not wanted, nobody likes me."

Both of these responses are extreme, and any profound feeling you get is entirely understandable. But what you do with them later on is what counts the most. Let's face it – whatever comes first to mind is what you truly believe in. However, while we are on the subject of identifying the automatic thoughts, we get a true insight into who we are. It is a type of awareness and understanding of your thinking.

Becoming aware is a process where you can distance yourself from the response you may have and reevaluate yourself. You start looking for the meaning in the situation and ask yourself whether there truly is the worst part about it and what it is. For example, in the example I mentioned earlier, if you have the ability to identify your automatic thought, specifically the negative one, the response would be "What's the worst part of it?" thus tapping into the core reason why you believe you are mistreated.

Recognizing the Connection Between Thoughts, Feelings, and Behaviors

What I personally love about CBT is that it has a unique way of uncovering the connection between thoughts, feelings, and behaviors. If you haven't noticed that by now, allow me to explain – the main goal of cognitive behavior therapy is to connect the three main dots – and allow you to see the full picture about yourself.

Has it ever happened to you that you act in a specific way and keep repeating that behavior? Have you ever concluded that you constantly have the same feelings and don't know why that's so? Shedding a light on your entire mindset is good – it gets you a step closer to change.

So, if the thoughts are ideas, feelings are the emotions you get after a thought occurs, and the behavior is the action you take as a result of the feeling, they seem pretty connected to each other, right? But how?

It is all about discovering whether you keep making the same decision over and over again. Take the example above – if you have noticed your friends going out for a cup of coffee without you often, and your first response was always a negative one, then ask yourself what you're feeling. Give it a moment to identify the emotion. If you are angry, ask yourself why. Slow down with the pace and pay attention to that little voice that's talking. What's it saying? Because this voice is you talking to yourself. Whenever you notice an automatic thought, here are a few questions that can help you make the connection – thoughts, feelings, behaviors.

What are your beliefs?

What is your self-talk?

What are your values?

What do you think about the people in that particular situation?

By recognizing this, you can determine whether the thoughts are realistic or not. Maybe, just maybe, the connection you make is only based on past experiences rather than an objective point of view. The connection between thought, feeling, and behavior will always happen, but it is your job to challenge your thoughts to be objective, and evidence-based rather than relying solely on the emotions, without knowing where that will take you (and let's face it – it's usually a negative direction).

Exploring the Cognitive Triad

The cognitive triad was developed as a framework by the founder of cognitive behavioral therapy, Aaron Beck. He wanted to create this as a scheme that would allow individuals to identify a negative pattern in their behavior easily.

This triad is (as you guessed it) a triangle with three specific points. It suggests that individuals who usually experience emotional distress are often negatively viewing themselves. However, they view the world and the future negatively, too. These are the kinds of negative feelings that arise from a place of anxiety, depression, and low self-esteem. As a teenager, it is your task to identify all of them so you can develop a more positive and realistic approach to life. To make things a little bit more visual for you, here is a figure of the cognitive triad.

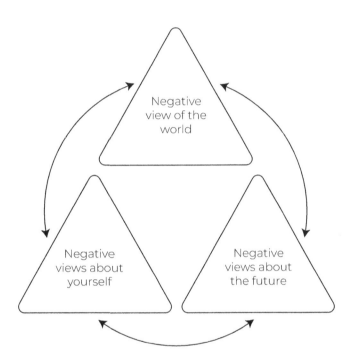

Here is a little example. The cognitive triad always starts with the self. In negative terms, it can represent a saying that you constantly use, such as "I'm never going to be good enough." The second corner of the triad is the views about the future. In negative terms, they can be something like "I will never achieve my goals." Finally, the last bit of the triad includes the views of the world. In negative terms, it goes something like this: "Everybody is out to get me."

While reading this, did one small part of your mind think these thoughts are most likely untrue? Did you find yourself in any of these statements? If that happens, you are on the right path to change. The cognitive triad is an excellent example of providing yourself with the mirror you need. It shows you how you have behaved so far, it shows you what your usual approach is, and it helps you become more aware of yourself and your negative thoughts.

With that in mind, I am giving you a moment to think. Notice your pattern of thoughts and actions, and then, identify the places where you believe you need improvement.

What Did You Learn From This Chapter?

Throughout this chapter, we went deep into the concept of self – once you made this realization that you are more than your thoughts and that there are a lot of dots to be connected, you learned the following:

- ✧ That there is a connection between thoughts, feelings, and behavior.
- ✧ How to identify the automatic negative thoughts.
- ✧ The automatic negative thoughts are normal, but only to a certain extent.
- ✧ Discovering that there is a connection between each part of who you are.
- ✧ Learning to challenge your thoughts whenever you notice it leads to a negative reaction.
- ✧ What is the cognitive triad, and why is it important.

Connecting the dots lifted a veil you didn't even know was there. You learned how everything within you works and that, just like the physical part (our bones are all connected), our thoughts are connected as well. I hope this made you feel a little bit better about yourself, yet you are still questioning how to solve this.

As I mentioned earlier in the chapter, negative thoughts happen all the time. Here, we recognized them and established a connection. In the next chapter, we will challenge them!

CHAPTER 03

CHALLENGING NEGATIVE THINKING PATTERNS

"Change your thoughts and you change your world." – Norman Vincent Peale

No truer words have ever been spoken. But, even with that in mind, people seem to neglect the fact that there is so much more to the act of challenging yourself. It takes great courage, persistence, and knowledge to stand up to probably the one person who gets in your way – yourself.

I have noticed, over my dedicated years of work, that teenagers are not aware of the power they hold within. As with every other adult on the planet, they also have the ability to control their thoughts. Yes, I am talking about you, too. I'm not sure whether the reason why they avoid doing this is because of fear they will fail or just plain laziness, but I am sure of one thing – you, and only you, are in charge of yourself. You are strong and capable, and after reading this chapter, you will know how to challenge negative thinking patterns.

Recognizing Cognitive Distortions

Here is the thing – you probably trust your mind too much. After all, is there anything else you can do? I mean, it is your brain at the end of the day, and it is probably right, right? Generally, it is a good idea to trust your brain. It is designed to look for your own good and find solutions or keep you away from dangers. But there are still situations where you might want to second-guess your trail of thought. Now, keep in mind here that your brain is not trying to trick you, lie to you, or deceive you; instead, it works this way as a result of developing some connections and beliefs that are not healthy.

This happens so often that it may surprise you. As I stated in the previous chapter, your thoughts, feelings, and behaviors are all connected, whether they make up for a good or a bad outcome. When the behavior is biased, that is how you define a cognitive distortion. The cognitive distortions are a representation of the irrational thoughts and beliefs that you constantly reinforce. As time passes, they become a part of who you are.

In the beginning, you may not notice them much – they are simply there – like a feature of your mind and your everyday thoughts. That is the reason why they are thought to be so damaging. You don't recognize them until they have completely taken over your mind. These cognitive distortions come in many forms, but they all result in inaccurate thinking patterns and false beliefs, and they have the potential to do some damage.

Now, it may be scary to admit this is happening to you – and that's perfectly normal. After all, you are human, and it is okay to fall under the spell of your own mind sometimes. We may all stumble occasionally, and some of us struggle with these challenges longer, and some don't. It is all about accepting the fact that some skills and abilities will only improve with practice, and they will help you become the best version of yourself. But let's not get ahead of ourselves.

To know exactly what to work on, you first need to understand how to recognize the cognitive distortions. Here is a list of the most frequent ones:

1. All or nothing – the polarized thinking also known as black-and-white thinking, where you go from one extreme to the next.
2. Overgeneralizing – the distortion where you generalize one example to an overall pattern.
3. Mental filter – focusing on the negative aspects of a situation, completely excluding the positive ones.
4. Removing the positive – a tricky situation where you acknowledge the positive aspects but completely reject them at the same time.
5. Jumping to conclusions – the inaccurate belief about what someone else is thinking, usually based on predictions without any evidence.
6. Catastrophizing – the act of stepping out of your perspective and exaggerating the meaning, likelihood, or importance of things.
7. Emotional reasoning – the realization that all of us have, at some point, experienced any one of these distortions.
8. Should statements – the statements you make about yourself and what you have to do.
9. Labeling – usually mislabeling – the tendency to go to extreme forms of overgeneralization, where you assign judgments of value to yourself and others.
10. Personalization – the situations where you take all things personally and blame yourself for no logical reason.

Recognizing cognitive distortions may seem a little scary at first, but it is all for the greater good. After helping these come to the surface, you can start implementing some techniques that can help you rewire your brain.

Techniques for Challenging and Reframing Negative Thoughts

Reframing negative thoughts may be challenging. Thankfully, there are many successful techniques that can help you achieve that. The techniques I'm about to share with you below can significantly change your overall outlook and mental well-being. Remember, the ultimate goal is not to completely remove the negative thoughts but to find a way to prevent them from overwhelming you.

1. Notice the negative thoughts. Pay attention to everything that pops into your mind. This could be anything – a situation, something about yourself, or something about other people.

2. Reflect and take a break. Identifying negative thoughts means taking a break and questioning whether your thoughts are accurate or not. This will not only lead you to the next step but will also prevent you from spiraling down into an unknown, dark maze of thoughts.

3. Think of the alternatives. When you realize that your thought is probably not true, consider other ways of viewing the situation. You can find both positive and neutral perspectives here and change your mind.

4. Replace the negative thought with a positive one. Once you pinpoint the initial negative thought, replace it with a positive or a neutral thought – and try to stick with it (mostly because it is probably the truth).

5. Stick with it. Any way that works for you is a good enough way to stick with a positive thought. You can be grateful for the work you've done that day, or you can write down your positive thoughts, or you can do any other thing that will help you feel empowered, and in control.

These techniques are amazing. When you start using them, in the beginning, it all may feel a little strange, but stick with it. After some time, you will see how helpful they are in the process of training yourself to be better.

The next exercises go into further detail on how to train your brain.

REFRAMING NEGATIVE THOUGHTS

Let's play this exercise called, "Fact or opinion?" During this exercise, you will have to sit and read through a list of statements that you will write yourself. These statements can be anything. Try to write at least ten of them, but if you have more, feel free to write all of them down. The statements should be your own thoughts - something that constantly pops into your mind. Below are some examples to get you started.

Now, put your thoughts on trial. Next to each of the sentences, write down whether you think they are facts or just your own opinion.

I am a failure. _____

I suck at everything. _____

I am ugly. _____

I rejected a friend when they asked for my help. _____

I'm a bad person. _____

I yelled at my parents. _____

Nobody cares about me. _____

Everything will turn into a disaster. _____

I am overweight. _____

I am selfish. _____

I am not loveable. _____

I failed an exam. _____

_____   _____

_____   _____

_____   _____

_____   _____

_____   _____

_____   _____

_____   _____

_____   _____

_____   _____

_____   _____

_____   _____

_____   _____

_____   _____

_____   _____

_____   _____

After doing so, look at the list again. Has anything changed? Your perception of yourself maybe? Did you notice that when you step back and objectively analyze your thoughts, most of them seem like they are just your opinions, and not reality?

You can take a breath now because, after this exercise, you know everything will be okay.

Creating Balanced and Realistic Thoughts

Balanced thinking seems almost impossible to achieve. You either go for the best or the worst-case scenario, right? Wrong.

Balance is something that should be incorporated into all aspects of your life. I can understand that, as a teenager, you might have difficulty achieving that, but the sooner you start training yourself, the better results you will have. Earlier, I mentioned that a part of the cognitive distortions includes seeing things in only black or white without giving the possibility for all the colors to shine through. Well, creating balanced and realistic thoughts is just that – the ability to see beyond the black and white and enjoy life while looking at things as neutrally and realistically as possible. It is like learning how to appreciate all the colors in the spectrum for the very first time.

It may sound a little less interesting at the moment, but there is a reason behind that, too – extreme thoughts can be exciting – and they usually are, especially for young people. But if you get used to this kind of behavior and abide by the rules of the extreme, it will eventually become a part of who you are.

By thinking in the middle, you get to see all the sides of a situation – sometimes there are two sides, sometimes more, but there is always more than one side. Cognitive behavioral therapy has ensured you can incorporate an approach that is not based on assumptions to get to the bottom of your thought trail.

Think about it – the balanced way of thinking is a calm way of thinking. It will provide you with benefits such as making better decisions, an overall state of calmness, less anxiety, being able to see the bigger picture, and so much more. Oh, and also, cognitive behavioral therapy is so much more than this, but you will have to stick around for the next chapters to find out!

EXERCISE 3

CREATING BALANCED THOUGHTS

To create balanced thoughts is easier said than done – that's why this exercise focuses on just that. It is called "the friend exercise," and here is what you need to do. Whenever you are faced with a challenging situation, something that might make you want to spiral down into that negative pattern you've adopted, first, write down your opinion about the situation and then, think about one of your closest friends. If you share your opinions and thoughts with them, how would they reply? What would they say? Write that down too.

Here is how the exercise would go:

Your opinion	Your friend's reply
I am really unhappy.	Is there a particular reason for that?
Everyone's ignoring me.	Have you reached out and noticed they do?
I don't get any attention.	What's the reason you need the extra attention?
I'm a bad person.	No, you're not, you're just having a bad day.
I'm not beautiful.	You are extremely beautiful.
Nothing goes well in my life.	Not true - you have plenty of things to be thankful for.
I am stuck in a loop.	One you can always get out of by making small steps.
I will never get better.	Yes, you will, and I am here for it.

X person doesn't like me anymore.

My terrible past will create a horrible future.

Have you tried talking to them and clarifying?

Not true - you are the creator of your future.

_____

_____

_____

_____

_____

_____

_____

_____

_____

_____

_____

_____

_____

_____

_____

_____

_____

_____

_____

_____

_____

_____

_____

_____

_____

_____

_____

_____

_____

_____

Their feedback will most likely differ from what you think. You don't even have to really share this with your friend – as long as you do the exercise, you practice a different point of view. After a while, you will realize that it is not so difficult to have several points of view about a certain thing – and the freedom to choose the most positive one.

Your thoughts are not always part of reality. Sometimes, the picture they paint in your mind differs from the truth – a lot. That's why this chapter focused on that – showing you how wonderful of a thing it is to have a few different opinions and the best ways to train your brain to look for the more positive in every aspect of life.

What Did You Learn From This Chapter?

✧ All the power you need to change is something you already hold within.

✧ Cognitive distortions are all around you; it is time to learn how to recognize them.

✧ A list of the most common cognitive distortions.

✧ Negative thoughts can be managed with a few well-utilized techniques.

✧ The realization that thoughts can be balanced.

At the end of the day, the sole reason why you picked up this book and decided to make it your ultimate guide toward change is because you want to be better. Once you figure out how to challenge your thoughts, it is time to put that work to some good use, don't you think?

In the following chapter, I will discuss how you can make more out of your trail of thoughts and influence them in a way that will lead to some spectacularly positive thinking – ultimately challenging yourself to improve your entire life.

Shall we? After you.

CHAPTER 04

BUILDING POSITIVE SELF-TALK

"It isn't what you have, or who you are, or where you are, or what you are doing that makes you happy or unhappy. It is what you think about." – Dale Carnegie

It takes some people a long time after they are born to realize that to be happy, you just need to be. It seems like the most essential things in life are also the most difficult ones to figure out. So, I understand where you are coming from. However difficult it may be to explain it, there is a certain lightness of being when you reach that state of positivity in your life. But to get there, you need to walk the path of building and realization.

In this chapter, we will commence our journey through the magnificence of indulging in positive self-talk together. Bear with me; it's not impossible to achieve, and if you think it is, allow me to change your mind.

Importance of Positive Self-Talk

There is something called "inner voice." This is a voice that only you can hear, and it is a way of talking to yourself. In many cases, you might not even be aware that you're doing it, but you still do it. This is a voice that combines your beliefs and thoughts and creates a sort of "internal monologue" that you "hear" during the day. As a concept, self-talk is a powerful thing because it has a big impact on who you are and how you feel. By underlining this, you realize its importance – ultimately knowing that it will either be a positive thing, something that will lift you, be supportive and beneficial, or turn into a negative thing and completely undermine your confidence.

Self-talk has a great impact on your mental health – the way you see yourself, and the way you view the world (the triad that I mentioned before). But the thing is, this can quickly turn for the worse if you don't know how to focus on the positive.

Negative self-talk can have a significant impact on your health overall – from chronic pain to affecting your confidence and creating a distorted body image; negative self-talk has many consequences. That is why we are solely focusing on the positive. The importance of positive self-talk comes from the fact that the benefits are – you guessed it, plenty. Here is only a handful of them:

✦ Improved self-esteem and overall wellbeing.

✦ Improved body image and less stress.

✦ Motivates you enough to overcome any challenges or obstacles.

✦ Reduces the symptoms of personality disorders, anxiety, and depression.

✦ Helps you feel in control of your life.

✦ Calms you down.

✦ Diminishes chronic pain.

Now, it sounds like something you want to try, right? We are headed toward the next exercise; take a look below.

PRACTICING POSITIVE SELF-TALK

Most people (especially the young ones) believe that practicing positive self-talk only limits your exposure to negativity. That is, to a certain extent, correct, but there is a lot more you can do in this situation. In this exercise, I am going to accentuate the power of self-care. I know self-care is something you see everywhere around you these days, especially because it is the talk of the town on social media. But have you ever stopped and wondered why that is so? Social media has a certain power; however, it is still not that great for many people. Nevertheless, the reach you can have with it makes up for a positive stamp you can leave in someone else's life. If you can do that, change the life of even one person for the better, why not try?

Now, let's see the exercise. I mentioned we're going to focus on self-care. The first thing you need to do is give yourself a small amount of time. Yes, start as small as possible – 5 minutes or 10 minutes of your day are enough to create a habit. Within this timeframe, do something for yourself. This is not a selfish act but rather a much-needed one. Engage in something that will lift your spirits and rejuvenate your entire well-being.

I can understand how the options may be plenty in this case, and viewing all of them may make you feel stuck rather than determined, so let's start from the beginning. Here are a few things you can do throughout your day:

✧ A little bit of physical activity.
✧ Focusing on a hobby of yours (painting, writing, cooking, etc.).
✧ Reading a book.
✧ Preparing a meal for yourself.
✧ Indulging in mindfulness meditation.

After doing any activity, the self-care bit comes later on. Take out a pen and write down three things that you liked about it below. These can be three good things you felt or thought, or whether the activity you engaged in put a smile on your face, made you forget about the time, etc.

The Activity _____

The Three Things I liked About It:

01. _____

02. _____

03. _____

The Activity _____

The Three Things I liked About It:

01. _____

02. _____

03. _____

The Activity _____

The Three Things I liked About It:

01. _____

02. _____

03. _____

The Activity _____

The Three Things I liked About It:

01. _____

02. _____

03. _____

The Activity _____

The Three Things I liked About It:

01. _____

02. _____

03. _____

The Activity _____

The Three Things I liked About It:

01. _____

02. _____

03. _____

The Activity _____

The Three Things I liked About It:

01. _____

02. _____

03. _____

The Activity _____

The Three Things I liked About It:

01. _____

02. _____

03. _____

The Activity _____

The Three Things I liked About It:

01. _____

02. _____

03. _____

The Activity _____

The Three Things I liked About It:

01. _____

02. _____

03. _____

The beauty of this exercise will come only if you are persistent. You won't notice an immediate difference, but after a while of indulging in this exercise, you will start noticing that positive self-talk is your "default setting." It is something your mind immediately jumps to, and it will help you train your brain to think in a healthier and stronger direction.

Identifying and Challenging Negative Self-Talk

I only scraped the surface on the topic of negative self-talk earlier. As a young mind, before we begin, what you need to understand is that negative self-talk is a part of being human. Just like positive self-talk can boost your productivity, improve your mood, and make you happier, negative self-talk has its consequences, too. It can diminish your self-confidence, it can lead to self-blame, and tear down your emotional well-being.

It is your responsibility to find the difference between having negative self-talk every once in a while, and constantly indulging in this pattern. Spotting the difference between the two is the first step toward making a change. It means you have identified the negative self-talk – and the second step is to dismiss it.

CHALLENGE THE NEGATIVE SELF-TALK

That leads us to this next exercise. I know that you want to make a change for the better. I know that you want to challenge yourself, your views, and the core of your beliefs. And in this exercise, that is exactly what you're going to do.

All of us are constantly met with negative thoughts during the day. These thoughts are either about yourself or your environment. But most of these usually pass after a minute or two. This is the correct way to deal with negative self-talk – acknowledge it, let it pass, and do not dwell on it. Once you notice that you are doing the exact opposite, turn to this exercise for help.

Here is what you're going to do.

Every time you notice that your mind is setting on a negative thought, and you find your inner voice saying, "You're not good enough," challenge that negative self-talk with positive self-talk. Keep doing this because persistence is a must for all change to occur.

There are many good things you can tell yourself, contrary to the negative belief that keeps popping up in your mind. Here are just a handful of statements for you to repeat each time you are faced with a negative self-talk pattern:

I will do my best.

I am good at this, and I can do it.

I will be well, and I will do well.

I am good enough.

I am happy, and everything is going well for me.

Below, you can find rows where you can write down your negative self-talk, and the positive self-talk you used to challenge it. Writing them down will significantly boost your progress.

Negative Self-Talk

_____

_____

_____

_____

_____

_____

_____

_____

_____

_____

_____

_____

_____

_____

_____

_____

_____

Positive Self-Talk

_____

_____

_____

_____

_____

_____

_____

_____

_____

_____

_____

_____

_____

_____

_____

_____

_____

Developing Affirmations and Positive Coping Statements

You have probably already noticed this – we are trying to create a positive mindset and cultivate mindfulness and happiness overall. Yes, there will be such things as bad days, but it is your responsibility to prevent them from ruling your life. Affirmations and positive coping statements are more than just a way to help you cope with a stressful situation or improve your mood. It can boost your self-esteem, it can help you look on the bright side of life, and most importantly, decrease negative thinking.

By using these affirmations and statements every day, you can work toward achieving the goals you have set for yourself and work on your overall personal development and growth. All of them are helpful every time you feel insecure or worried or when you need a little push. I know it sounds strange to talk about affirmations at the moment; it may even sound silly to some of you, but that is exactly why you should try them.

Many people undermine the power of affirmations because they seem "too easy." Well, if they are too easy, why not give them a try? Positive thinking has always been effective and beneficial for improving alertness and mindset and effectively coping with every curveball life throws at you.

The idea is – when you constantly repeat these to yourself – whether they are about your body, your mind, your relationship with yourself, your environment, etc, they will become engraved in your mind. After a while, you will truly start believing them and, as a result of that, think more positively.

Not quite sure how to make that happen? I prepared two exercises below so you can differentiate between affirmations and positive coping statements so that you can learn how to implement both of them in your life.

AFFIRMATIONS

This exercise comes in the form of journaling. While you may not be up to the idea at first, hear me out. When you put pen to paper and write down your affirmations, it will seem like they have taken a certain shape, like they make sense, that there is truth to them. That is why this exercise is an extremely powerful one.

Your first step is to take out a pen (and a notebook if you prefer writing to it rather than to the lines below). Then, you are going to choose some affirmations that "make sense" to you or some affirmations you'd like to embed in your mind. You can find some affirmations either in books or online, or you can come up with them yourself. To get you started, here are a few:

I am strong, and I always attract positivity.

———o–◇–o———

I can heal, and I can only attract healthy things into my life.

———o–◇–o———

I am grateful for everything in my life right now.

———o–◇–o———

I am kind, and I am enough.

———o–◇–o———

I see the beauty that lies within me.

———o–◇–o———

I create my own future.

———o–◇–o———

Only good things will happen to me.

———o–◇–o———

_____

_____

_____

_____

_____

_____

_____

_____

_____

_____

_____

_____

_____

_____

_____

_____

_____

_____

_____

_____

_____

_____

_____

_____

_____

_____

_____

Keep writing these affirmations – either one in a day or all of them (depending on how you feel). After some time, you will notice that your self-talk will consist of plenty of affirmations that instantly put a smile on your face.

POSITIVE COPING STATEMENTS

This next exercise is all about focusing on positive coping statements. These are the ones that you can use every time you feel sad or down, something that will help you cope with difficult times. The difference between the previous exercise and this one is in the approach – because basically, you do the same thing – repeat positive things to yourself. But, in the previous exercise, the idea is that you approach affirmations with a neutral mindset. Here, with positive coping statements, you approach the exercise because you have noticed a negative pattern of thoughts in your mind (usually caused by an external event).

So, here is what you need to do. We have all been there – a stressful situation creating a chain of negative self-talk, and whether it is a mild or a severe reaction, it still needs to come to an end. That is when the coping mechanisms come into play. When you are faced with this kind of situation, you can remember and repeat one (or a few) of the following positive coping statements:

This is not final; it will pass.

———o–◇–o———

Stop, give yourself a minute, breathe – because you can do this.

———o–◇–o———

Even if I am feeling angry, I can still deal with this.

———o–◇–o———

Feeling bad is a normal reaction, but I will allow it to wash over me and pass.

———o–◇–o———

It is something I have done before, and I will do it again.

———o—◇—o———

It will not last forever.

———o—◇—o———

I don't need to rush. I can take things slowly.

———o—◇—o———

My mind is not always my friend.

———o—◇—o———

I feel this way because of past experiences, but I should feel okay now.

———o—◇—o———

I am stronger than I think.

———o—◇—o———

I learn from experiences, and I see every challenge as an opportunity.

———o—◇—o———

Things will be easier next time.

———o—◇—o———

Repeating these statements to yourself each time you are faced with a challenging situation can help you easily move forward and cope with whatever comes your way in a healthier way.

What Did You Learn From This Chapter?

Having to learn a lot about positive self-talk means tapping into the core of who you are and realizing that you have a good side – something light and happy to accentuate. With that in mind, here is an overview of what you learned in this chapter:

- ✧ What is self-talk, and what is the importance of positive self-talk.
- ✧ What is negative self-talk, how to identify it, and what it can do to you long-term.
- ✧ What are affirmations and positive coping statements, and why they are important.

Positive self-talk is the pillar to creating a better and stronger you. This chapter was filled with enlightenment and richness, and it may have even put a smile on your face. However, deep down, you still feel like you can't do this... like you need something more to make this happen and change your life for the better. It seems like the catalyst you're looking for to start this process is still lost.

That's what the next chapter is all about – the catalyst you are looking for is called acceptance, and it is one you need to work on before you continue your journey through the magnificence that cognitive behavioral therapy brings. You have me by your side every step of the way, so don't even try to get discouraged! Instead, turn the page, and let's start working on that together!

CHAPTER 05

MINDFULNESS AND ACCEPTANCE

> *"The curious paradox is that when I accept myself just as I am, then I can change."* – Carl Rogers

When it comes to mindfulness, the beginning is always the most challenging part of it. Somehow, it seems like being present at the moment is both the easiest and the most challenging thing to do. To tell you the truth, almost everything in this book will initially feel that way. But that should not stop you from going after what you want to achieve.

Since this is the chapter where you might have the most questions, I decided to focus it on practice rather than theory – because sometimes, the best way to learn is through exercise. It is time to focus on mindfulness and acceptance.

Introduction to Mindfulness

Allow me to start answering all of your questions in this first bit. Let's start with the easiest thing – do you know what mindfulness is?

Mindfulness is the ability of an individual to be fully present and aware of the moment, where they are going, what they are doing, and refrain from being overly reactive or overwhelmed by the surroundings. Usually, mindfulness is something that everyone possesses naturally, but some people have a better grip on it than others. Do you know why that is so? It's because these people practice it daily. Now comes another question – how do you practice mindfulness daily? What can it do to make your life better?

When you bring mindfulness into your life, you start feeling it through all your senses. Mindfulness is a state of mind through which you can wake up the emotional, mental, and physical processes within you. It is available to you at all given moments; all you need to do is pause, breathe, and allow it to settle in.

There are many mindfulness techniques you can try. By utilizing the techniques below, you can improve your mental clarity and stray as far away from anxiety and negative thought patterns as possible. Some of them may seem a little strange to do at first but trust me on this one – you will find that all of them are successful in the end. But before we go directly into the techniques, let's talk a little bit about acceptance and non-judgemental awareness.

Cultivating Acceptance and Non-Judgemental Awareness

Cultivating acceptance and non-judgemental awareness is not particularly a different subject in itself but rather another aspect of mindfulness. Now, let's take things a step back. We live in a world where jumping to conclusions and judgments happens all around us. The practice of non-judgemental awareness and acceptance seems to fade away slowly. Instead of being the norm, it has become the exception to the rule. That is why it is of utmost importance to explore the significance of being calmer and centered and approach everything in life with less judgment and a more accepting mindset.

To understand non-judgment, you first need to understand the nature of judgment. This is a cognitive process through which you classify, estimate, and then form opinions about yourself, other people, ideas, situations, etc. The way you do that is through your core beliefs and morals. Judgment is a natural part of being a human, but it can easily turn into an issue when you are using too much of it.

Contrary to that, we have non-judgment. Cultivating this can help you view situations and events from multiple perspectives. When you remove judgment from the equation, you provide space for empathy and a deeper understanding. This process promotes effective communication and a healthier way of dealing with everything that happens around you.

But the best part about it by far is enhancing growth and moving in a positive direction. Approaching yourself and the people around you with acceptance and non-judgment means creating a new terrain to walk on – a terrain of growth. This means allowing yourself to move past your vulnerabilities, insecurities, and mistakes and then fostering a mindset that focuses on development and freedom of expression.

All of this may sound like the best thing you can do, but none of it would be possible without using these practical strategies and the exercises below. Let's go over the strategies together before moving on to the exercises.

1. Try to cultivate mindfulness. As I mentioned at the beginning of this chapter, mindfulness is the practice of being completely present in the moment – but you need to achieve that without any judgment. This way, you can reflect and choose a better and calmer response.

2. Challenge your opinion every time – especially if it is a hypothetical one. Judgment is often based on limited information, so every time you find yourself in this situation, challenge your thoughts. Seek out a different perspective, have an open dialogue with different people, and be open to changing your mind and broadening your horizons.

3. Empathy is key. This shows the ability to understand the people around you without immediately turning to judgment. You put yourself in their shoes, and you show genuine compassion.

4. You avoid using stereotypes – about yourself and the people around you. Stereotypes are conceptions (or misconceptions) about a certain individual based on a larger group of people. Stereotypes can limit your understanding and lead to judgment rather than acceptance.

5. Reflecting upon your past self is like challenging your beliefs, impulses, and judgments. See how your behavior history has developed and what you want to change about it. By examining your own impulses, you can work toward creating a less judgmental approach.

6. Indulge in non-comparison. You don't need comparison in your life. Not because it frequently leads to judgments but because it is an arbitrary way of examining yourself. Instead of comparing yourself to others, why not concentrate on your growth? You will get a lot more out of it by doing so.

FIVE SENSES MINDFULNESS

We are starting with the exercises, with the five senses of mindfulness being the first one. As an exercise, it has proven to be incredibly helpful, especially in cases when you want to completely feel like you are present at the moment. This is a practical way to practice mindfulness fast in any situation. All you need to do is follow the instructions. Here they are:

5 Notice five things you can see. Take a good look at your surroundings and bring to your attention five things that you can see. Out of everything that you see, choose something that you normally wouldn't pick.

4 Notice four things you can feel. No matter what your surroundings look like, try to find four things you can feel. This can be anything from the texture of your clothes to the surface of a chair, a table, a sofa, or anything you can find.

3 Notice three things you can hear. Take a moment to shut down all your other senses and notice three things you can hear. These, too, can be anything that surrounds you – from the traffic outside on the street to the birds chirping, to a clock ticking, to someone talking loudly in the background, to the sound of the rain.

2 Notice two things you can smell. This is an important one, as it needs a lot of concentration. No matter what is inside the room, you need to isolate the other senses and focus on the things you can smell – be these pleasant or unpleasant smells. Maybe it's a nice perfume, maybe it's the food from the next room, maybe it's the smell of the rain.

1 Notice one thing you can taste. This is when you can go for the food you've smelled a few minutes earlier. If that is not the case, focus on anything else you can taste – a beverage, a taste in your mouth, a piece of gum – anything.

This is a very easy way to achieve a state of mindfulness. You don't need a lot of time to do it, but you can still be aware of yourself and the current moment.

BODY SCAN MEDITATION

This exercise is like doing an x-ray on your entire body. Get started and sit in a comfortable position. Focus on that, and then shift your focus to your breath. Notice the sensation you have each time your lungs fill with air and each time you exhale. Then, choose one part of the body from which you can start. It can be either the top of your head or the bottom of your body (left or right foot). Be careful, pay attention, and focus on that particular spot. Spend about 20 seconds to a minute focusing on that particular spot before you move on to the next part of your body. Acknowledge the sensation that is happening when you focus on each individual part, and don't forget to breathe in and out through each step in the process. The deep breaths can help you relax and release the tension in your mind and body.

During this exercise, it is okay for your mind to drift a little. Notice that, and when it happens, slowly return your thoughts and focus to the present moment. Remember, if this happens, you haven't failed or anything because you can always bring the thoughts back to your body and move on. If it helps, visualize how you get the thoughts back before continuing.

This awareness exercise can help you maintain your focus on a certain thing, thus helping you be more present in the moment.

BOX BREATHING

This is a very quick and easy way to get yourself into a calmer state. As an exercise, it is something that anyone can practice, especially in cases when you want to bring back your thoughts and keep your concentration. Here are the steps you need to take:

1. First, breathe in through your nose, and count slowly to four while you do. Focus on the present moment and feel how the air fills up your lungs.

2. Then, hold your breath for about 4 seconds. Avoid inhaling or exhaling during this time.

3. Then, slowly exhale through your mouth for a duration of 4 seconds.

4. Wait 4 seconds until you inhale again.

5. Repeat this process 4 times - that's enough to help you to center yourself.

MINDFUL WALKING

There is a certain awareness that happens each time you walk. This awareness can help you observe your impulses, emotions, and thoughts, as well as sensations that run through the body. As an exercise, mindful walking can help you develop positive behavioral change and develop coping skills. Here are the three steps of this exercise:

✧ Prepare yourself to go out for a walk. Before you start walking, try to stand still for a few moments and focus on your breathing. Notice how every part of your body feels.

✧ When you begin your walk, try to notice every movement of each part of your body. Notice how everything feels - your arms, your legs, your head, your skin, every part of you. Notice how you carry your body around.

✧ Once you've done that, start paying attention to everything around you. If you feel like your thoughts are getting distracted, slowly bring them back to the present moment. In the end, how did the walk make you feel?

ACCEPTANCE PRACTICE

The highs and lows in life are unavoidable things, and the sooner you understand that, the better grasp you will have of yourself. I can understand that, as a young person, you don't quite know how to handle situations where you just have to accept yourself, a situation, or a moment. That is why I am proposing this acceptance practice exercise. You'll find this to be especially useful in situations where you're not particularly satisfied with an outcome. Here is what you need to do:

1. Describe the situation you're in right now to yourself. Now answer this - what about that situation makes you unhappy or dissatisfied?

2. Has this situation happened before? If so, how did you react to each time it happened? Did you look for help, did you look for acceptance, or were you angry and hopeless?

3. If you could do something to change the situation, what would that be? What do you think is holding you back to make this change? Or, if you have no other choice but to accept the situation as it is, what do you think is holding you back from surrendering to it?

4. The final question you're going to ask yourself is connected to the future. To remain present, how will you approach this situation from now on?

Take this as an example - you're feeling helpless, like you are in a vortex, and you want to get out of it immediately. Start answering the questions above (honestly and truthfully) and see where they lead you. To help you start thinking in the right direction, here are a few starting points. When you have found yourself in one of the situations below, this is the best exercise to use.

Situation: A grade on a test

Reaction: _____

Can you change the situation? How?: _____

_____

_____

_____

How will you approach this the next time?: _____

_____

_____

_____

Situation: Your favorite sports team lost a game

Reaction: _____

Can you change the situation? How?: _____

_____

_____

_____

How will you approach this the next time?: _____

_____

_____

_____

Situation: A social event where you didn't "deliver" as good as you hoped you would

Reaction: _____

Can you change the situation? How?: _____

_____

_____

_____

How will you approach this the next time?: _____

_____

_____

_____

Situation: A falling out with a friend or at home, maybe with your parents or guardians

Reaction: _____

Can you change the situation? How?: _____

_____

_____

_____

How will you approach this the next time?: _____

_____

_____

_____

Situation: A creative project gone wrong

Reaction: _____

Can you change the situation? How?: _____

_____

_____

_____

How will you approach this the next time?: _____

_____

_____

_____

Situation: _____

Reaction: _____

Can you change the situation? How?: _____

_____

_____

_____

How will you approach this the next time?: _____

_____

_____

_____

Situation: _____

Reaction: _____

Can you change the situation? How?: _____

_____

_____

_____

How will you approach this the next time?: _____

_____

_____

_____

Situation: _____

Reaction: _____

Can you change the situation? How?: _____

_____

_____

_____

How will you approach this the next time?: _____

_____

_____

_____

Situation: _____

Reaction: _____

Can you change the situation? How?: _____

_____

_____

_____

How will you approach this the next time?: _____

_____

_____

_____

Situation: _____

Reaction: _____

Can you change the situation? How?: _____

_____

_____

_____

How will you approach this the next time?: _____

_____

_____

_____

GRATITUDE PRACTICE

Feeling bad is pointless – someone had to say it. I figured, why not me? This last exercise for this chapter focuses on how to do more than accept a situation in your life but rather celebrate it. I know it seems a bit strange to do that, especially if you find yourself in a situation you don't like, but this exercise can help you realize one thing. That even if you are in an unwanted spot at the moment, in the grand scheme of things, you are right where you're supposed to be – and you should be thankful for that.

Let's simplify it – here's what you need to do for this exercise:

✧ Describe yourself as you are at the moment or a situation you're in at the moment that you don't really like.

✧ Think about this for a while – even if you are not in a particularly good situation, how can you benefit from it? There has to be something good about it, but you never gave it much thought. So, in this case, give it a moment and give it the thought.

✧ Before you wrap up this exercise, find one (or a few) different perspectives from the one you have. Remember – feeling pointless about something is normal, but to a certain extent. As a young person, you have the power to appreciate the opportunities and benefits of every thought, feeling, and situation and use them to feel better and act on something.

✧ Finally, what can you do to express gratitude for the situation you're in at the moment? (there has to be something)

Let me give you an example of this. You wake up in the morning, and everything seems okay. You're making yourself a good breakfast and you want to savor it before your day begins. But you burn the breakfast and make a mess out of the kitchen. You start thinking that everything always goes wrong, that you're good for nothing, and that everything is a mess. Once you feel the onset of these thoughts coming, just pause for a while and allow them to pass through you. Among the chaos, find at least one thing you're grateful for - the sun, the cold, the fact that you're standing in the kitchen, still learning how to cook, apparently, the fact that you're alive and well, and these things happen to anyone - it can be anything. Give power to that rather than giving power to the momentary negative feelings you have.

Situation: _____

How can I benefit from it?:

1. _____

2. _____

3. _____

Things I am grateful for:

1. _____

2. _____

3. _____

Situation: _____

How can I benefit from it?:

1. _____

2. _____

3. _____

Things I am grateful for:

1. _____

2. _____

3. _____

Situation: _____

How can I benefit from it?:

1. _____

2. _____

3. _____

Things I am grateful for:

1. _____

2. _____

3. _____

Situation: _____

How can I benefit from it?:

1. _____

2. _____

3. _____

Things I am grateful for:

1. _____

2. _____

3. _____

Situation: _____

How can I benefit from it?:

1. _____

2. _____

3. _____

Things I am grateful for:

1. _____

2. _____

3. _____

Situation: _____

How can I benefit from it?:

1. _____

2. _____

3. _____

Things I am grateful for:

1. _____

2. _____

3. _____

Situation: _____

How can I benefit from it?:

1. _____

2. _____

3. _____

Things I am grateful for:

1. _____

2. _____

3. _____

Situation: _____

How can I benefit from it?:

1. _____

2. _____

3. _____

Things I am grateful for:

1. _____

2. _____

3. _____

Situation: _____

How can I benefit from it?:

1. _____

2. _____

3. _____

Things I am grateful for:

1. _____

2. _____

3. _____

Situation: _____

How can I benefit from it?:

1. _____

2. _____

3. _____

Things I am grateful for:

1. _____

2. _____

3. _____

Situation: _____

How can I benefit from it?:

1. _____

2. _____

3. _____

Things I am grateful for:

1. _____

2. _____

3. _____

Situation: _____

How can I benefit from it?:

1. _____

2. _____

3. _____

Things I am grateful for:

1. _____

2. _____

3. _____

These exercises are more than just a mechanism to help you cope with yourself and your environment – they are the arsenal you need to become better, stronger, and healthier.

What Did You Learn From This Chapter?

This is a chapter where you managed to reach deep within – and uncover a calmer and more centered side of you. Other than realizing that every one of us has it, you learned the following:

- ✧ What is mindfulness and an introduction to a few techniques.
- ✧ What is acceptance and how to cultivate non-judgemental awareness.
- ✧ Learned an exercise about the five senses of mindfulness.

Mindfulness and acceptance should be a core part of who you are. They can help you walk the path of calmness and control of your life. Speaking of control, it still feels like you haven't reached that point where you can have complete control of your behavior patterns, right? Fear not, because, in the next chapter, I am starting the subject of understanding those behavior patterns – taking a step toward grasping the steering wheel of your life. Turn the page, and I hope you're ready because you're in for a wild ride!

PART

02

CBT BEHAVIORAL TECHNIQUES

CHAPTER 06

UNDERSTANDING BEHAVIOR PATTERNS

"Small daily improvements are the key to staggering long-term results." - *Anonymous*

No matter what you do in life – be that personal development, professional development, or any other aspect of your life – it can be improved if you are consistent and work on it daily. Cognitive behavioral therapy is here to show you just that. With me as the vessel, you get to learn new things about yourself with every new chapter.

We all have certain behavior patterns. These affect us in a certain way and are our personal characteristic traits. It is a chain of thoughts and actions that have happened in certain patterns within your life, and they have often repeated themselves over and over. In this chapter, you will notice that I am focusing on two specific aspects – the ABC model and the triggers that lead to impulsive behaviors. Finally, we will wrap up this chapter by learning how to identify behavior patterns.

Exploring the ABC Model – Antecedents, Behaviours and Consequences

The ABC model is a perfect example of how CBT works – focusing on the present rather than the past. This basic CBT technique assumes your beliefs based on how you react to certain events. As a model, it challenges cognitive distortions and irrational thoughts. That, in turn, allows you to reconstruct these thoughts or beliefs into healthier ones.

This model has many benefits for your mental and emotional health. By using the ABC model, you can identify inaccurate thoughts and beliefs and learn how to let go of them. The process itself teaches you how to notice your automatic thoughts. However, instead of immediately acting upon them, you get to give yourself a break and explore different options. Once you see how it works, you will notice that you can use it in many situations – be that with yourself and your private thoughts, in a professional environment, or whenever you come face to face with a challenging situation.

Before I move on to the exercise where you can see the ABC model in motion, remember one thing about it – it can help you develop positive emotions and rational thoughts. So, each time you're faced with anxiety, anger, embarrassment, guilt, fear, or sadness, this is the model to turn to.

THE ABC MODEL IN USE

This model's beauty is that you can pinpoint a negative thought whenever you have it. Things immediately make more sense when you try to shape them in a certain way. In this case, they are shaped into letters. Before you begin this exercise, you should know the components of this model. Here they are:

- ✧ **A** – means the activating event or adversity
- ✧ **B** – means your beliefs about that certain activating event. These beliefs include both obvious and underlying thoughts about yourself, others, or a certain situation
- ✧ **C** – means consequences. These consequences usually include your emotional or behavioral response

Now, when you start the exercise, you work under the assumption that the letters A, B, and C are connected, and B is the most important component. CBT as a concept focuses on B to change the thinking patterns and create new ways of viewing yourself, the people around you, and situations.

Think about it this way - A is the activating situation or moment, B is your beliefs and thoughts about this moment, and C is the consequences of those beliefs.

For example, (A:) your friend agrees to have lunch with you, but they don't follow up on the initial agreement. Your mind immediately jumps to a conclusion (B:), thinking that they don't care about you, and then (C:) you start blowing things out of proportion with the thoughts that nobody cares about you, pick a fight with your friend, and so on.

Your exercise is to think of a situation when something similar to this happened to you and analyze how you reacted to it. When you come up with the situation, start from the very beginning - point A. Only this time, you will try to come to a different outcome. What happened at point A? Sit with that for a while and try to think of exactly what happened.

To come to point B, recognize your thought patterns and all the irrationality around them. Recognize that they make you have negative feelings and are part of a vortex you thought you couldn't get out of – until now. Come up with different approaches and different patterns of thoughts - more positive ones - that will lead you to different conclusions. Abandon the thought you originally had at the moment when the situation occurred and look for alternatives.

When you finally arrive at point C, it means you've done everything to explore other options for your specific situation and have managed to shift your thoughts. They are now neutral or positive, realistic, and don't make you feel angry or sad as a response to them.

Sit with this for a little bit. Learn how you can apply this exercise in various situations. Here are a few examples you can get started with:

1. Instructions given to you by your parents. They do that a lot and you don't really like it.

2. The feeling of peer pressure. It feels like everyone is doing much better than you.

3. Having an exam in the near future. The pressure of the "deadline" before the exam is too much to handle.

4. A reminder that you need to come back home before X o'clock. You don't need a reminder that you're still a teenager.

5. A warning from a teacher. This can lead to the school contacting your parents.

6. Social media. Either too much of it or not enough of it can make you feel anxious.

Antecedent (**A**): _____

_____

_____

Behavior (**B**): _____

_____

_____

Consequences (**C**): _____

_____

_____

Antecedent (**A**): _____
_____
_____

Behavior (**B**): _____
_____
_____

Consequences (**C**): _____
_____
_____

Antecedent (**A**): _____
_____
_____

Behavior (**B**): _____
_____
_____

Consequences (**C**): _____
_____
_____

Antecedent (**A**): _____

_____

_____

Behavior (**B**): _____

_____

_____

Consequences (**C**): _____

_____

_____

Antecedent (**A**): _____

_____

_____

Behavior (**B**): _____

_____

_____

Consequences (**C**): _____

_____

_____

Antecedent (**A**): _____

_____

_____

Behavior (**B**): _____

_____

_____

Consequences (**C**): _____

_____

_____

Antecedent (**A**): _____

_____

_____

Behavior (**B**): _____

_____

_____

Consequences (**C**): _____

_____

_____

Antecedent (**A**): _____

_____

_____

Behavior (**B**): _____

_____

_____

Consequences (**C**): _____

_____

_____

Antecedent (**A**): _____

_____

_____

Behavior (**B**): _____

_____

_____

Consequences (**C**): _____

_____

_____

Antecedent (**A**): _____

_____

_____

Behavior (**B**): _____

_____

_____

Consequences (**C**): _____

_____

_____

Antecedent (**A**): _____

_____

_____

Behavior (**B**): _____

_____

_____

Consequences (**C**): _____

_____

_____

Antecedent (**A**): _____

_____

_____

Behavior (**B**): _____

_____

_____

Consequences (**C**): _____

_____

_____

Antecedent (**A**): _____

_____

_____

Behavior (**B**): _____

_____

_____

Consequences (**C**): _____

_____

_____

Antecedent (**A**): _____

_____

_____

Behavior (**B**): _____

_____

_____

Consequences (**C**): _____

_____

_____

Antecedent (**A**): _____

_____

_____

Behavior (**B**): _____

_____

_____

Consequences (**C**): _____

_____

_____

With those newfound thoughts and emotions, how would your behavior change? Do you notice it taking a turn for the better?

Recognizing Triggers for Impulsive Behavior

Many people believe that impulsive behavior is a disorder. I am here to tell you that just because you've been stuck in the maze of your mind doesn't mean you are dealing with a disorder. However, you should still know how to manage your impulse control and avoid impulsive behaviors.

An impulsive behavior is every time you act quickly on something without any thought about the consequences. In your mind, only the present moment exists (which is a good starting point), but there is no thought about the future whatsoever. What young minds such as yourself fail to notice here is that we all act on impulses sometimes. It is a part of who we are, and it is an important part of the human experience. But, if you indulge in this behavior for a longer period, instead of only engaging in it from time to time (until you become an adult and learn how to control it), then it means you are walking a thin line.

When you are acting on impulse, it means you are acting spontaneously. You don't consider how it could affect you later on or how it could affect others. You never wonder what might happen because you only think about the here and the now.

Before I move on to the exercise, I am sharing a few examples of impulsive behavior. You may recognize yourself in some, and that's okay because here, I have created a safe space for you to learn and develop at your own pace.

Here are the examples:

- ✧ You have frequent outbursts
- ✧ You overshare details of your personal life with everyone you meet
- ✧ You overindulge in things, showing binge behavior
- ✧ You tend to make all situations a lot scarier and more urgent than they actually are
- ✧ You turn to hurting yourself, physically, mentally, or emotionally, every time you are faced with disappointment.

COMMON TRIGGERS

Every day, you experience a wide range of emotions – be those positive, neutral, or negative. Almost all of them relate to a certain event, something that happens to you that day. However, it is your response to these events that matters. These events are your triggers, and you act on them based on a similar previous experience. It encompasses your state of mind based on past memories, experiences, or events, and it usually results in an intense emotional reaction, no matter what your current mood is at the moment.

This exercise can help you know your common emotional triggers and how to deal with them so you can create and maintain good emotional health.

Take out a pen and dedicate some time to sit with yourself. Think about some situations that made you feel bad. Which part of those situations triggered you? Was it some kind of disapproval, rejection, or exclusion, or maybe you felt ignored, critiqued, unwanted, smothered, insecure, and like you were losing control? These situations are known as common triggers, where you lose your independence and turn to something you're not. Once you pinpoint the feeling, listen to your mind and body. Your mind is probably loud and filled with negative thoughts, and your body also shows symptoms – a pounding heart, shakiness, and sweaty palms.

Some of the most common triggers young people face are fear of rejection, stress, being ignored, negative memories, being ridiculed, conflict, psychological trauma, being vulnerable, helpless, having a lack of socializing, etc.

Now go ahead and write everything down below:

Situation

The Trigger of Bad Feeling

_____

_____

_____

_____

_____

_____

_____

_____

_____

_____

_____

_____

_____

_____

_____

_____

_____

_____

_____

_____

_____

_____

_____

_____

_____

_____

_____

_____

_____

_____

_____

_____

_____

_____

This is when you need to take a step back and acknowledge your current state, but remember, that you know the root and know how to get there and change the reaction. Remind yourself that it is okay to feel whatever you feel, but let it pass through you. Own your feelings, but do so with compassion for yourself, not judgment. Give yourself some space, take a short break to regroup, and return to the situation with a calmer mindset.

Identifying Patterns of Behavior

At the end of the day, you started reading this book so you can not only improve yourself but learn how to accept yourself. For without acceptance, there is no change. It can be difficult to accept that you are dealing with something that is a core part of who you are, but by identifying that part of you, you give yourself the unique chance of improving the situation – improving yourself.

It all comes down to being self-aware and acknowledging a pattern. In this case, whatever happens, I would suggest one thing – that you commit honesty toward yourself. Be honest about every feeling and every thought because you need a certain recognition to strengthen your mind. Identifying your pattern of behavior will do just that – push the subconscious act into the realm of consciousness, where you are fully aware of what is happening to you. Apply logic to this case, and you know that you can shift or tone it down whenever you notice a behavior pattern with a negative frequency. By doing this, you create new opportunities for self-reflection and growth.

Self-Regulation Workbook for Teens

What Did You Learn From This Chapter?

It is important to realize that you have so much power within you – and that you can easily take control of yourself. But everything seems so much easier once you find out the perfect steps to make that happen. In this chapter on understanding behavior patterns, you learned precise ways to deal with yourself, among other things, as pointed out below:

✧ What is the ABC model and how it can influence your thinking patterns.

✧ What is impulsive behavior and its triggers.

✧ How the common triggers are connected to your behavior patterns.

When you understand your behavior patterns, that's when all things start to put themselves into perspective. With this, you go through the process of opening up to yourself, right down to your core, to find out what you're truly made out of. When you get that out of the way, only one thing remains: start building yourself up! To do that, you will need to develop a few skills, the first of which is coping skills. I am here to help you achieve that – turn the page because the next chapter is all about it!

CHAPTER 07

DEVELOPING COPING SKILLS

"We cannot solve our problems with the same thinking we used when we created them." – *Albert Einstein*

What does it mean to cope? It seems like, every day, you are coping with something, and everything feels like it is out of the ordinary. Each experience gives you a different thought, each action creates a reaction within you, and each feeling you have, comes with a set of consequences. The thing is, you noticed that you focus more on the negative rather than the positive. You start feeling like your mind and spirit are both tumbling down. You know, throwing a pebble down the side of the hill will ultimately nudge larger and larger rocks along the way. By the time it all reaches the end, some large rock formations would have fallen.

If you are coping with some emotions and thoughts that cannot be explained any other way than this, it is time for you to learn how to put them aside. In this chapter, I am teaching you all there is to know about effectively managing yourself. The best way to do that is by developing strong coping skills.

Learning Effective Coping Strategies for Managing Stress and Emotions

Negative emotions and stress can sometimes get the better of you. That's understandable to a certain extent, given the lifestyle most of us lead. Even for a young person such as yourself, things can feel a little too much sometimes. But noticing that you have more stressors in life than good feelings is the first step in the right direction. The second is implementing some effective coping strategies.

The main purpose of these strategies is to learn how to tolerate negative events and realities while keeping your positive self-image and emotional control intact. You implement coping strategies each time you face a life challenge. This challenge is usually a negative situation and requires some sort of adaptation on your end. Other times, some positive changes may make you feel stressed, too. All of them require you to adapt and adjust to a certain new environment or situation, and for a brief moment, until you do that, you might feel like you don't have control over the situation. That may make you feel bad, panicked, anxious, or depressed. In some cases, it can even go to extremes. You are here because of that – so we can push the negative aside and learn how to deal with it. By learning these coping strategies, you will learn how to glide smoothly through life rather than trip and fall every time.

To manage your emotions and stress every time, here are some effective coping strategies for you:

- ✧ When faced with a situation, instead of jumping to conclusions, try to find as much information about it as you can. If necessary, include the people in your support group and find a solution.

- ✧ Any problem can be broken down into small parts. That way, instead of dealing with it as a whole, you deal with smaller, more manageable chunks.

- ✧ Practice breathing and relaxation techniques. They will automatically regulate your nervous system and keep you calm.

- ✧ Don't underestimate the power of a creative outlet. Anything from art, music, or dance can help you healthily process your emotions and be a productive way to spend your time.

- ✧ Get in touch with a friend who makes you feel like you are loved for who you really are.

- ✧ Reach out to a mentor, parent, or teacher – anyone who can guide you further.

- ✧ Work on reframing your negative thoughts and shifting your mindset. Remember, it is all about looking at a situation from a different point of view.

- ✧ The power of journaling is no joke. When you write things down, you put them into perspective, and they start making sense in terms of what you're going through. But they are also easier to handle once you physically see them in front of you.

- ✧ Dedicate your time to helping someone else. When you indulge in such an activity, you can help lower your overall stress levels and connect to others. Ultimately, you work on your well-being and health.

Whenever you feel like you want to react negatively in a given situation, remember that there will be consequences to that. Once you start gathering these consequences, one by one, they will come up to be the core of your personality - since you would be reacting to them, thinking about them, and so on. Since both positive and negative behaviors are repetitive patterns, it is high time you've learned the coping skills for each situation. The next step is building a "toolbox" of the coping skills you've mastered the most.

Building a Toolbox of Coping Skills

Okay, so let me ask you something – what do you do when you're emotionally activated? We all indeed have different ways of coping with stress, but what are your "go-to" tools that you take to deal with an unwanted or stressful situation? If you're reading this book, that means you either want to update your skills or you want to change them completely. As a young adult, trying this on your own may be difficult because you don't have a starting point.

But now, with this book, you can easily focus on building a toolbox of coping skills.

What is a toolbox of skills? These are the skills you have up your sleeve and you use them each time you are faced with a challenging situation. However, before you build your own toolbox, you need to learn something. The key to developing new skills and knowing how to use them is practicing them even when you're not emotionally activated. Once you develop that ability to think clearly in any situation, things will seem a lot easier to cope with. This is something you can rely on each time you move forward and overcome a curveball.

To move on and try to implement those skills in your daily life, you need to decide what you're going to put in your emotional toolbox first. As you are starting from scratch, here are a few suggestions to get you started. You can use these skills every time you feel like you need soothing.

1. **Distract yourself** – there is nothing wrong with distracting yourself every time you feel upset. If you start feeling like you can't keep control over a certain situation, and you don't want to let go of control, then it is most likely best if you step back. Distract yourself with something until the strong emotions pass. This is only the first skill you can implement, so try to combine it with some of the other skills that I mention below. Here, you can watch a movie, listen to music, get into a hobby of yours, do some puzzles, etc.

2. **Mindfulness exercises** – whenever you're feeling emotionally overwhelmed, it is difficult to focus on the present moment. Your mind wanders all over the place, and it is challenging to stay put in the present. That is why mindfulness exercises are a perfect thing. These exercises can help you shift the attention back to yourself and to where you are right now and how you're feeling right now. The exercises can be anything you want – from a breathing exercise to meditation exercise, journalling, coloring, or maybe even progressive muscle relaxation exercises.

3. **Move your body** – by moving your body, you keep the mind active in the present, so this is another skill you should keep up your sleeve. You don't have to do extreme exercises here; all you need to do is listen to your body and go at your own pace. Sometimes, intense movements are what you need. Other times, you can focus on slow movements. This can be anything – from stepping onto your yoga mat to running, gardening, stretching, or doing some exercise videos.

4. **Calming sensory objects** – using your senses to calm down is a great way to keep yourself grounded and in the present moment. In this case, you can, for example, touch something or engage a few of your senses at the same time. If you are faced with a challenging situation, look around you – that's the first thing that will keep you in the present. Find some sensory objects. These can be a soft blanket, a candle, a lotion, a pen, a toy, a fidget spinner, a warm or cold beverage, a piece of gum, photos of people – it can be anything.

It is such a happy feeling to create a palette of coping skills and keep them up your sleeve just in case a challenging situation arises. This so-called toolbox can help you stay more calm and centered - because you know that, at any given moment, you have something to fall back on rather than falling into a hole of negativity. After this, it is time to learn how to implement these coping skills in day-to-day situations.

Implementing Coping Skills in Daily Life

It is all about dedicating some time out of your day to give something to yourself. Working on yourself is very important, and since you picked up this book, you're already on the right path. But you still need to put in some effort.

For most young people, time management is a challenging concept in itself. Every day has 24 hours, and how you divide your time and attention is what matters the most. Once you subtract the time for rest, time to finish your daily obligations, and time spent with your friends and family, there is rarely some time to focus on yourself, right? Well, the first thing you're going to do is learn how to manage your time and give at least five or ten minutes during the day to yourself. Even in those times when you feel like you are racing with the clock, pause for a second, breathe, and start over.

When you look at it from a different perspective, it is about priority management more than time management. If you want to put in the work and create a better version of yourself, then you need to dedicate minutes, if not hours, to yourself only.

Be careful though, your mind may trick you into believing that self-care is selfishness. That dedicating time to yourself is a bad thing. Don't trust that voice. You are being kind and compassionate to people and yourself. You are working to achieve a certain goal. You are starting a journey to self-care and self-revelation.

So, create a schedule first. You already have the coping skills listed above, and you know you need to work on them every chance you get, not only in a situation where you're emotionally challenged. Now, all you need to do is begin. Implement the coping skills we uncovered in your daily life. Soon enough, you will notice yourself exhibiting a different pattern of behavior. A better one.

What Did You Learn From This Chapter?

The purpose of this chapter was to open your eyes to the world of possibilities. To teach you about all the things you can do and be and how to cope healthily with everything life throws at you. To summarize, here is what you learned from it:

✧ Some effective strategies that can help you manage your emotions and stress levels.

✧ A set of coping skills you should have in your arsenal.

✧ How to implement those coping skills in your everyday life.

Coping skills are easy to master. I know that after the end of each chapter, you are baffled by all the new information you learn, but as you can see, the next chapter always completes the previous one. Using that logic, things will seem a lot easier once you delve into the next chapter – which is all about behavioral activation. Turn the page and learn all about it!

CHAPTER 08

BEHAVIORAL ACTIVATION

"Do not wait, the time will never be 'just right.' Start where you stand, and work with whatever tools you may have at your command, and better tools will be found as you go along." – George Herbert

There is an idea that focuses on enhancing a sort of positive behavior. Behavioral activation is just that – deliberately practicing certain behaviors to activate a positive emotional state. The concept depends on the fact that as long as you engage in good and healthy activities, you will feel good.

How does this seem to you? Is it something you would try? When I was young, I thought this would never work for me. But, despite my doubts, I still gave it a go. After a few failed attempts, I focused on enhancing my behavioral activation. So you see, this is something anyone can do. And I bet that you would be better at it than I was! Do you want to know why I think that? Because you have this book in your hands!

Understanding the Connection Between Behavior and Mood

Remember that I mentioned the relationship between thoughts, emotions, and behavior in the previous chapters. Now, in order to change that, you need to acknowledge and recognize it first.

I want us to begin by distinguishing between emotions and feelings. These are often confused with each other, yet they are pretty different. Now, don't get me wrong; they are still connected, but they come with different time limits and labels. By understanding the difference, you will be able to better control your behavior and make healthier choices in life.

Emotions. They are not conscious. These reactions happen within your body, and they often come as a consequence of thoughts, memories, and experiences. Some of the most common emotions include happiness, anger, sadness, fear, surprise, and disgust. Also, emotions are often associated with facial expressions.

Feelings. On the other hand, feelings happen in the mind. They are conscious. They are a reaction to the emotions you are experiencing. Feelings are based on the reaction to the emotions you are experiencing, as well as the perception of any events and thoughts.

Emotions and feelings are two separate things because emotions happen due to a physical response within the brain, and feelings are a response to the emotional reaction.

So, how can these two impact your behavior?

Because the emotions create a physical response, and the feelings are conscious, they impact your overall behavior. However, in such situations, people tend to believe that their behavior is justified because of their emotions. The thing is, as long as they believe this, they may struggle to understand that behavior is a choice. Behavior does not have to be impacted by your mood. Behavior can be healthy. Once you start noticing this, you can make a change. If your mood often dictates your behavior, you can react in three ways – positively, negatively, or refuse to respond at all. If you allow your emotions to control your behavior, then you live on so-called "autopilot." That kind of behavior may lead to you making choices you will regret later. As long as your behavior is based on your feelings, it can lead you astray.

MOOD AND ACTIVITY DIARY

Let's do an exercise here. Get a pen and locate the worksheet below. Have them handy at all times during the next week or so. Within this timeframe, try to notice your mood every time – when you get up in the morning, before you go to bed, at each time during the day, and every time you come face to face with any type of situation.

Always take a minute to reflect and write down your mood and behavior. As I have already mentioned, when you put anything on paper, it takes a form of its own and becomes more real. Think of you writing down how you felt as a sort of diary. Once the week has passed, you can go back to your notes and see how your mind has gradually shifted for the better, even if it is a little bit.

Activity: _____ Mood: _____

Activity: _____ Mood: _____

Activity: _____ Mood: _____

Activity: _____   Mood: _____

Activity: _____   Mood: _____

Activity: _____   Mood: _____

Activity: _____   Mood: _____

Activity: _____   Mood: _____

Activity: _____   Mood: _____

Setting and Achieving SMART Goals

The reason why I'm adding this as a segment into this book is because it is important to know how to work on your goals, not just to have them. In your case, you are working on creating a better, calmer, and happier self. But, sometimes, everyone needs a little push in the right direction. That's why I am including the SMART goals.

Whatever you put your mind to, you can achieve. Think of the SMART goals as your guide that will help you get to where you want in a specific timeframe. For those of you who are already familiar with this concept, let's revisit it. And for those of you who don't know it, take a look at it below:

SMART is an acronym that can help you determine your goals – make them reachable and clear, as they should be. Here is what every letter stands for:

S – stands for specific, significant, simple, and sensible

M – stands for measurable, motivating, and meaningful

A – stands for achievable, attainable, and agreed

R – stands for relevant, realistic, result-based, and reasonable

T – stands for time-bound, time-based, timely, and time-sensitive

While this sounds simple and straightforward enough, you probably still need some guidance on how to practice it. That's why we are moving on to the next exercise.

SMART GOAL-SETTING

The goal you want to achieve now is to adhere to positive behavior and change a certain aspect of yourself that will affect the quality of your overall lifestyle. With that in mind, here is how to set a SMART goal.

This approach is based on certain criteria. Take a pen and write down your goal. Then, find the SMART letters in a vertical line below it. Add your answers to the following questions next to each letter -- see below.

S > be specific. What will you achieve? How will you do that?

M > be measurable. What will you use as a pointer to show you that you've met your goal?

A > be achievable. Do you possess the right skills to achieve this?

R > be relevant. How important will the results be?

T > be time-bound. What is the deadline for you to achieve your goal?

MY GOAL

_____

_____

S _____

_____

_____

M _____

_____

_____

A _____

_____

_____

R _____

_____

_____

T _____

_____

_____

MY GOAL

_____

_____

S >
_____

_____

_____

M >
_____

_____

_____

A >
_____

_____

_____

R >
_____

_____

_____

T >
_____

_____

_____

MY GOAL

_____

_____

S > _____

_____

_____

M > _____

_____

_____

A > _____

_____

_____

R > _____

_____

_____

T > _____

_____

_____

MY GOAL

_____

_____

S > _____

_____

_____

M > _____

_____

_____

A > _____

_____

_____

R > _____

_____

_____

T > _____

_____

_____

MY GOAL

_____

_____

> **S**

_____

_____

_____

> **M**

_____

_____

_____

> **A**

_____

_____

_____

> **R**

_____

_____

_____

> **T**

_____

_____

_____

MY GOAL

_____

_____

S >
_____

_____

_____

M >
_____

_____

_____

A >
_____

_____

_____

R >
_____

_____

_____

T >
_____

_____

_____

MY GOAL

_____

_____

S >
_____

_____

_____

M >
_____

_____

_____

A >
_____

_____

_____

R >
_____

_____

_____

T >
_____

_____

_____

By learning that the SMART goal will provide you with clarity, motivation, and focus, you can soon learn to implement it with every other goal you have – not just this one.

Increasing Engagement in Positive Activities

Science has always suggested that positive thinking is a skill everyone can learn. It is also the main focus of this book. But when it comes to actually doing the work, a lot of people shy away from it. Before thinking that it "takes too much work" to do it, think about the near future. Visualize yourself doing things you want, things that make you feel complete and happy. Just the thought of it makes you happy, doesn't it?

Well, think about how much better you will feel if you actually increase your engagement in positive activities. Just stop and think about what makes you happy. Do you have a hobby that makes you feel fulfilled? Do you have an interest that makes you lose track of time? It can be anything – as long as it puts a smile on your face. It can be drawing, going out with people, watching a movie, reading a book, meditating, running, or photography – all cards are on the table!

By increasing engagement in positive activities, you learn how to stay present in the moment. Your mind does not wander around, creating negative scenarios and falling into the same depressing vortex over and over again. Rather, it instead focuses on what you can do better. As insignificant as this may sound in the beginning, indulging in such activities can help you shift your mindset after a while.

BEHAVIORAL ACTIVATION WORKSHEET

I have found that the most successful way to indulge in behavioral activation is by making a worksheet. Trust me, it is as simple as it can get. There is not much complexity to it, and you don't even have to dedicate a lot of time to it. A few minutes of your day is enough.

Take a pen and write down all the things you love. I mean, things you truly love. They can be of any area of your life. For example, you can write the following.

I love my pet.

I love that I get up early every morning.

I love that I work on myself at least once a week.

I love that it's summertime.

I love watermelon.

You see? This can be anything as long as you focus on the good things. There is always something good and something to be thankful for, and by indulging in this exercise, you accentuate it.

_____

_____

_____

_____

_____

_____

ACTIVITY EXPERIMENT

The next exercise for today is focused on the question – *what would you do if you knew the* <u>*outcome*</u> *would be the best possible scenario?*

Experiment with a particular activity. Say you want to improve your mood and focus; running three times a week is an excellent way to do that. But you feel like you're going to fail as soon as you begin. Well, I am all up for changing your thoughts, so let's do it. I know that if you've never run before, your mind will immediately go to thinking you'll fail. Let's entertain that thought for a minute. Why do you think you will fail? Because if you never ran before, how would you know? True, you need to have a certain level of physical preparedness to run, but you also need to run to have physical preparedness. It is a circle, and one cannot go without the other.

Once you realize this is the same for all activities you want to indulge in, you will start looking at it a bit more positively. For the sake of this exercise, let's look at the best possible scenario. You will start running three days a week. You will feel incredible, you will look better, and while you're thinking about your future self, you always picture yourself with a smile on your face. That's the best-case scenario I want you to focus on every time you want to start something new. It doesn't have to be running exactly – it can be anything you want as long as it is an activity that will make you happy.

Activity: _____

The Best-Case Scenario: _____

_____

_____

_____

Activity: _____

The Best-Case Scenario: _____

_____

_____

_____

_____

Activity: _____

The Best-Case Scenario: _____

_____

_____

_____

_____

Activity: _____

The Best-Case Scenario: _____

_____

_____

_____

_____

Activity: _____

The Best-Case Scenario: _____

_____

_____

_____

_____

Activity: _____

The Best-Case Scenario: _____

_____

_____

_____

_____

Activity: _____

The Best-Case Scenario: _____

_____

_____

_____

_____

POSITIVE ACTIVITY CATALOG

This last exercise for this chapter is connected to the previous one. After you do your best with the smallest positive activity and you see the results, you will want to do another activity and then another one. As you stack these up, one at a time, you end up creating a catalog of everything you're doing to improve yourself.

All you need to do here is to remember to write everything down. Write down the activity, how it made you feel, and how often you indulged in it. This is sort of a journalling process except we call it a catalog of positive activities. Give it a few months to really see the results. Let's say you've indulged in several activities in the past period, and then you stopped to look back on how far you've come. Everything you've written down will be the catalog you refer to – each time you need inspiration or a little boost to move ahead in life.

Activity: _____

How it Made me feel?: _____

_____

Times done: ☐   ☐   ☐   ☐   ☐   ☐   ☐   ☐   ☐   ☐   ☐

———o–◇–o———

Activity: _____

How it Made me feel?: _____

_____

Times done: ☐   ☐   ☐   ☐   ☐   ☐   ☐   ☐   ☐   ☐   ☐

Activity: _____

How it Made me feel?: _____

_____

Times done: ☐ ☐ ☐ ☐ ☐ ☐ ☐ ☐ ☐ ☐ ☐ ☐ ☐

———o–◇–o———

Activity: _____

How it Made me feel?: _____

_____

Times done: ☐ ☐ ☐ ☐ ☐ ☐ ☐ ☐ ☐ ☐ ☐ ☐ ☐

———o–◇–o———

Activity: _____

How it Made me feel?: _____

_____

Times done: ☐ ☐ ☐ ☐ ☐ ☐ ☐ ☐ ☐ ☐ ☐ ☐ ☐

———o–◇–o———

Activity: _____

How it Made me feel?: _____

_____

Times done: ☐ ☐ ☐ ☐ ☐ ☐ ☐ ☐ ☐ ☐ ☐ ☐ ☐

———o–◇–o———

Activity: _____

How it Made me feel?: _____

_____

Times done: ☐ ☐ ☐ ☐ ☐ ☐ ☐ ☐ ☐ ☐ ☐ ☐ ☐

Activity: _____

How it Made me feel?: _____

_____

Times done: ☐　☐　☐　☐　☐　☐　☐　☐　☐　☐　☐　☐　☐

———o–◇–o———

Activity: _____

How it Made me feel?: _____

_____

Times done: ☐　☐　☐　☐　☐　☐　☐　☐　☐　☐　☐　☐　☐

———o–◇–o———

Activity: _____

How it Made me feel?: _____

_____

Times done: ☐　☐　☐　☐　☐　☐　☐　☐　☐　☐　☐　☐　☐

———o–◇–o———

Activity: _____

How it Made me feel?: _____

_____

Times done: ☐　☐　☐　☐　☐　☐　☐　☐　☐　☐　☐　☐　☐

———o–◇–o———

Activity: _____

How it Made me feel?: _____

_____

Times done: ☐　☐　☐　☐　☐　☐　☐　☐　☐　☐　☐　☐　☐

Activity: _____

How it Made me feel?: _____

_____

Times done: ☐   ☐   ☐   ☐   ☐   ☐   ☐   ☐   ☐   ☐   ☐   ☐   ☐

———o–◇–o———

Activity: _____

How it Made me feel?: _____

_____

Times done: ☐   ☐   ☐   ☐   ☐   ☐   ☐   ☐   ☐   ☐   ☐   ☐   ☐

———o–◇–o———

Activity: _____

How it Made me feel?: _____

_____

Times done: ☐   ☐   ☐   ☐   ☐   ☐   ☐   ☐   ☐   ☐   ☐   ☐   ☐

———o–◇–o———

Activity: _____

How it Made me feel?: _____

_____

Times done: ☐   ☐   ☐   ☐   ☐   ☐   ☐   ☐   ☐   ☐   ☐   ☐   ☐

———o–◇–o———

Activity: _____

How it Made me feel?: _____

_____

Times done: ☐   ☐   ☐   ☐   ☐   ☐   ☐   ☐   ☐   ☐   ☐   ☐   ☐

What Did You Learn From This Chapter?

Slowly but surely, you are learning so much about yourself and how you can improve. This chapter was probably a true revelation that there is always a flip side to everything. By learning this now, you keep in mind how to be more assertive and engage in positive behavior.

Let's review what we've learned from here:

- ✧ Explaining what behavioral activation is.
- ✧ What are emotions and feelings, and how they differ from each other.
- ✧ Behavior can be a consequence of feelings, but behavior is always a choice.
- ✧ Setting SMART goals.
- ✧ Increasing engagement in positive activities makes you more present.

It is very easy to let negative emotions and feelings control your behavior. That's probably the reason why most people indulge in it. It takes perseverance, control, and determination to get to the other side – where the grass is greener. I am breaking down the journey into small steps to make things a lot easier for you, and I hope you can already feel the difference! But, as much as I like to say that we're almost there, you still need to do a few things. The next chapter is all about assertiveness training. With it, you will unlock a whole new level of yourself. What are you waiting for? Turn the page!

CHAPTER 09

ASSERTIVENESS TRAINING

"The only limit to our realization of tomorrow will be our doubts of today." –
Franklin D. Roosevelt

Train your brain – that's all you ever need. In the previous chapters, I focused on the importance of looking at thoughts, feelings, and behavior as one. But now, it is time to focus only on the aspect of assertiveness. This will be the tool that will keep you in check every time life gets complicated.

Before we delve into the chapter together, let's talk about assertiveness – do you know what it is? Assertiveness is the quality of being confident and self-assured without being hostile or aggressive. Many people think this is a part of personality, which is why some people have it while others don't. The truth is that this is a skill that you can train yourself to possess. The assertiveness skills can help you respond to any situation better and help you build yourself up into a stronger version of yourself.

Importance of Assertive Communication

Since this is our subject for the chapter, and I have dedicated an entire one to it, why is it so important? Assertiveness, in itself, is something quite a lot of people struggle with. As a young person, you may feel like you fear hurting someone else, appear selfish, show aggression, etc. All of these are reasons why you feel afraid to be confident, to stand up for yourself, and to voice your needs.

In many situations, these fears come from a lack of understanding about assertiveness. To clear things up right from the start, assertiveness is not to be mistaken with aggression – even though both include showing your point of view. The difference is that aggression has a hostile and demanding approach, and assertiveness includes calm and respectful communication.

By explaining them, you can see how important assertive communication is. You will show stability to yourself first and then to the people around you. Then, you will know how to ask for something with confidence and clarity. Finally, you will stop feeling subjugated and powerless and instead step into your full force.

Learning Assertiveness Skills

Rather than boring you with details and theory, I want to focus on practice within this chapter. You are fully aware of what assertiveness is. Now, it is time to start learning how to implement it in your life. Learning assertiveness skills is one of the most effective ways for you to get your message across. Here is how to learn assertiveness:

✧ **Think about your style** - are you a more active person, someone who wants their voice to be heard, or are you a more passive person, and tend to stay in the background? Once you determine this, it is time to apply the next steps.

✧ **Use first person singular** - whenever you want to talk about something, use "I" as much as you can. This will give off the feeling that you're using statements that connect you, meaning you are ready to take on responsibilities or consequences.

✧ **Learn how to say no** - this is very self-explanatory. If you don't want to do or say or feel something, just say no.

✧ **Rehearse** - if you have something to say, and you're afraid you're not going to sound right, rehearse it.

✧ **Body language** - at all times, you need to be aware of your body language - for it speaks even when you keep quiet. Notice yourself in front of the mirror - and practice poses that are calm and radiate certainty.

✧ **Check on yourself** - the last step and the biggest one is checking in on yourself. Your emotions and your thoughts are what matter the most, so at all times, keep them in check. There's no need for you to give off what you think and feel all the time. Instead, take a deep breath, take a step back, and calmly approach every situation.

Actually, learning assertiveness seems easy, right? But why would you learn it if you don't know what you're gaining from it? Understandable. I wouldn't want to abide by anything if I didn't know how it would help me. With that in mind, here is what you will gain from learning assertiveness skills:

✧ Better communication – when you are being assertive, you have the best chance to successfully deliver a message across. If you are too much on the aggressive side, then you are more likely to lose the message in the process, as the receiving party will only focus on the aggression they see. It is all about being honest about what you want.

- ✧ Increased confidence and self-esteem – when you truthfully communicate your feelings and thoughts, you stand up for yourself, your rights, and the core of who you are. This naturally boosts your confidence and self-esteem.

- ✧ Improved relationships – starting from the relationship you nurture with yourself, moving on to your relationships with the people around you. Assertive communication is usually based on mutual respect and trust, and that is why it is an important aspect of every relationship. Communicating directly and being honest can eliminate any resentment or underlying negative feelings that come from a point of unmet needs.

- ✧ Less stress – this is my favorite benefit. We are all aware that stress is an unavoidable part of life. But did you know that not putting yourself first can elevate your daily stress levels to uncomfortable heights? A lot of stress for a prolonged period leads to significant changes within your mind and body for the worse. Also, learning to be assertive can make you feel stressed. However, while being more assertive may make you feel discomfort and tension initially, knowing that you are open and straightforward in your communication while considering all parties involved will significantly decrease your stress levels long-term.

Improving your communication abilities does not have to come with a high cost. Sometimes, all it takes is to focus on yourself and learn a few new skills.

Role-Playing Assertiveness Response

Before I go into the exercises, one last bit. Being able to communicate assertively is a skill you need to develop so you can maintain healthy relationships, both with yourself and the people around you. It also helps build up your self-esteem.

Role-playing assertiveness response is assertiveness training. Through it, you get to experience all sorts of things – how you initially want to react when you're met with an uncomfortable situation and how to train your brain to react in a more assertive way.

To understand this in-depth, take a look at the exercises below.

ASSERTIVE COMMUNICATION ROLE-PLAY

This exercise is focused on role play. Learning how to communicate assertively is best done by switching sides. Let's say you are talking to your parents or guardian, and they say that you need to focus on yourself and start standing up for yourself. While this seems reasonable for a parent to say, you act out. You begin to shout and say that you don't want to do anything, that you constantly feel pressured, and you don't know where to begin so you can make yourself better.

With the assertive communication role-play, you switch the roles any way you want. You can either be the parent and understand their point of view and why they are discussing this with you. Or you can indulge in assertive feedback rather than aggression. Either way, this assertive communication exercise is developed to help you change your point of view and teach you how to react more calmly in such challenging situations.

ASSERTIVE COMMUNICATION SCENARIOS

The last exercise for this chapter is connected to assertive communication scenarios. In these scenarios, try to think of something that already happened just to see if you could have reacted better in that situation. Assertive communication scenarios can be truly helpful if you want to retrace your steps back and see how far you've come, or to see how much more you need to work on.

Let me give you a few examples of these assertive communication scenarios.

✧ For example, you can start with the feedback you received. It can be anything from feedback at home to feedback at school etc. Something that made you have negative feelings.

✧ Or you can move on to declining something you don't want to do. Maybe there has been a situation where you have felt pushed into doing something you didn't want to do, which made you act out later on. We are all human, and when we're cornered, aggression can quickly surface.

✧ Criticism is next. You can see it everywhere you go. Sometimes, you even feel it deep down. But oftentimes, it happens that criticism is something we don't take lightly. This especially goes for young people. It can make you feel helpless, and it can make you act out.

These are only a handful of situations where you might have felt like you are doing less than optimal work, or that you're cornered, or you simply feel attacked, and you have the need to fight back. Well, let's turn that around.

Here are 10 scenarios for you to practice. Some of these situations may have already happened to you, while others may not have. For those that you've already experienced, you could try practicing how you would have altered your behavior. Also, for those you haven't experienced, try to think of how you would react in the best possible way.

1. You felt cornered by your classmates for who you are.
2. You had a verbal altercation with someone.
3. Your parents looked at you at dinner, and it felt like there was disappointment in their eyes.
4. You woke up from a bad dream feeling terrible, and that feeling persisted throughout the day.
5. You find yourself thinking that you'll never be good enough.
6. Your teacher confronted you for a lousy job you've done on your homework.
7. People make fun of you because of a certain hobby you have.
8. Every time you look in the mirror you don't like what you see.
9. You voiced out an opinion with your friends, and they laughed at you for it.
10. The feedback you got for a project you worked on was not what you expected it to be.

Now, think of how you already reacted earlier, or think about how you would react in each one of these situations (it was probably not optimal). The next step is to replay that scenario in your mind, but this time, try to turn your reaction around. Instead of bursting out, what would you say to make your response assertive?

Looking back on these types of communication encounters and how you could have improved them will help you better understand the great role assertiveness has in your life. It will also help you look at any situation with a clear mind and readiness to communicate and solve anything that comes your way!

What Did You Learn From This Chapter?

Assertiveness is a skill that will serve you throughout your life. A little bit of theory and a lot of practice can go a long way. Let's review what we learned from this chapter:

- ✧ What is assertive communication.
- ✧ The importance of assertive communication.
- ✧ What you will get by learning assertiveness skills.
- ✧ How to role-play an assertiveness response.

By looking at the logical order of things, once you know how to approach a certain situation in life, you should know how to solve it, too, right? Life gives us challenges every day, and the best way to deal with them is to go toward them – head-on. So, the following chapter will focus on that. I know that you probably already possess some problem-solving skills, but it is time to take a deeper look into it. Let's turn the page and continue learning.

CHAPTER 10

PROBLEM-SOLVING SKILLS

"A problem is a chance for you to do your best." – Duke Ellington

I love that you have picked up this book in your hands because, by this stage, you are pretty much aware of the power within you and how you can do your best at any given moment. We talked about the many challenges you might face and how to identify them, and I added many exercises that can help you get back on the right track.

This chapter offers an entirely different insight into yourself. While I helped you tap into your emotions and feelings in the previous chapters, we will discuss matters of the mind here. Your true power comes from your thinking patterns – if you focus on reshaping them, you focus on creating a better you.

Now, we're delving deep into the subject of problem-solving and how it can help you reform yourself.

Steps for Effective Problem-Solving

The problem-solving skills are an absolute must when it comes to skills you should work on. Once you step out in the world, you will see that having these skills will make the difference between success and failure in everyday situations. These skills can help you navigate the complexities and challenges of life and get accustomed to the ever-changing environment.

But what encompasses effective problem-solving? Is this something you are born with, or something that you can develop over time? You're just in luck because these skills can be developed at any point in life – but as I say, the sooner, the better. Whenever you find yourself in a situation that requires a solution and you don't know where to begin, turn to problem-solving. This can be anything that happens during your day. It can also be anything that happens within you. As we work together to get you up and running, learning the steps that will help you get there is important. Now, I will only mention these steps, and we will discuss them in detail below.

I like to consider these the ultimate five steps to tackling any challenge in your life. These five steps consist of:

1. Identifying the issue
2. Generating all kinds of possible solutions
3. Evaluating those solutions
4. Implementing the chosen solutions
5. Adjusting as necessary

Now, let's break these down and talk about them, one step at a time, starting from the top.

Identifying Problems and Generating Solutions

The first step in the problem-solving process is to have a clear definition of the challenge, issue, or setback. You don't need to do this in an instant. Remember, some situations are a little more complex and require a longer time to decipher them. That's okay. During that period, collect as much information as you can. Because the more information you have, the better and easier it will be for you to identify the cause of the issue at hand. For example, if you constantly succumb to negative thoughts, it is essential to identify where it comes from and how it affects you. Also, it is necessary to underline that it all comes from a lack of training. Once you clearly understand the root cause, you can start developing a solid action plan to address it. It is highly important to include all available information – gather first, act on it later.

By doing this step, you are doing yourself a favor – as you are directly affected by the situation.

By doing this, you take a step back to gain a different perspective and insight.

The second step is all about brainstorming. Finding a few possible solutions to a challenge can sometimes be more difficult than you can imagine. I urge you to stay on course and be persistent, as it is worth it in the end. I would advise that, as soon as you come to this second step, you try to come up with as many solutions as you can. It doesn't matter if they are very unrealistic or not. The point of this step is to teach yourself how to stray from your regular mindset. Brainstorming and generating all sorts of possible outcomes can help you bounce off ideas. Once you delve into deep thinking, you can create such a session that the ideas you generate will be amazing, and you can just keep them in the back of your mind without any judgment or critique. Coming up with a list of possible solutions may take a while or a bit. It all depends on your specific way of functioning. Consider all the options you have thought of and weigh the pros and cons of each option. Given the information you gathered, what seems like the most effective solution to you (out of all the things you came up with)?

Evaluating and Implementing Solutions

The question leads us to the third step, which is evaluating the solutions. Within this step, it is crucial to keep an open mind and always consider a different perspective. Try to step out of your usual way of thinking as much as you can. Take all the time you need during this process, especially in the beginning, because you will need some time to train your brain anyway. While you are on this step, it is important to consider the consequences of all the options you have in mind. Some of the long-term effects may not be up to your liking. That is why you are in the process of evaluating each possible option. Prioritize them based on their feasibility and the impact they may have. While they sound nice in theory, their execution may be more challenging than you can imagine, while other solutions may be instantly implemented. That is why choosing a solution that addresses the challenge directly and effectively is essential. If you need some help in this section, you can always go back to the SMART concept to help you out. The last thing to remember here is that not all may work according to plan, and you should always keep this in the back of your mind – but more on that later.

The fourth step is implementing the solution. Here is when you need to start planning carefully. Everything needs to go as smoothly as possible, and you must know your responsibilities. Designing a layout plan with everything in front of you will give you a better idea of how to execute it. You can see this below in the exercise 25, solution implementation practice.

Monitoring, Adjusting, and How the Overall Process Will Make You Feel

Last but not least, it is always important to track the implementation process. As this is the last step of your problem-solving skills, you can only truly complete this process once you realize that regular check-ins are a must. While you are implementing a solution to any of life's challenges you're faced with, it is vital to address them from time to time to prevent them from becoming bigger or creating an additional challenge. Adjusting the solution is imperative to ensure that whatever you want resolved is on the right track. Sometimes, plans don't go as they're supposed to, and you may end up with a problem that is not fully resolved. The thing is, you need to be flexible while you approach a challenge or an issue. Monitor how your chosen solution works, and if you feel like something could be done better, don't be afraid to make any adjustments. It all comes down to the feedback you get – both from yourself and your surroundings. The solution should completely resolve the issue and fulfill your hopes. Once you notice this is not happening, it is time to take actionable steps. Take a few steps back. If necessary, go to the brainstorming step, and see what else you've come up with. Maybe things will change when you look at the solution from a different perspective. And you will find that something else may work better instead.

It is important to be fully invested in the process. This five-step problem-solving process can help you overcome any obstacles you face. Remember that it is all about defining the problem, analyzing it, and getting all the necessary information – those are the first steps. Then, by understanding the root of the issue, you come up with a few solutions and go for the one that seems the most logical at the moment. If by any chance something doesn't work out, back to the drawing board you go!

I love it when people are being practical about something. That's why I tend to focus on creating the ultimate mind-spirit balance. But, to do that, we always need exercise. The following exercises you see will provide you with an incredible way to get in touch with yourself and activate that problem-solving part of your mind.

PROBLEM-SOLVING STEPS PRACTICE

Another way to name this exercise is "a real-life example." You need to practice the problem-solving steps over and over again. In this first exercise, I encourage you to start doing this whenever you are faced with a challenge because there is no better way to master problem-solving skills than to begin utilizing them right there – on the spot!

Depending on your situation, you may have to wait a little longer for such a situation to arise. If that's the case, then give this practice a nudge. Think of any past situation that has been haunting you for a while now. Write it down. From this perspective and this point in time, how would you approach it? Write that down too. Now that you have more knowledge in your arsenal, would it be easier for you to tackle it? Why? Also, once you've settled it in your mind, how did that make you feel? Follow the problem-solving steps below and start practicing.

1. Identifying the issue.
2. Generating all kinds of possible solutions.
3. Evaluating those solutions.
4. Implementing the chosen solutions.
5. Adjusting as necessary.

1. The Problem: _____

2. Possible Solutions: _____

_____

_____

_____

_____

3. What is Good/Bad in Each of the Solutions?: _____

_____

_____

_____

_____

_____

4. The Solution I Will Implement: _____

_____

_____

_____

_____

_____

1. The Problem: _____

2. Possible Solutions: _____

_____

_____

_____

_____

3. What is Good/Bad in Each of the Solutions?: _____

_____

_____

_____

_____

_____

4. The Solution I Will Implement: _____

_____

_____

_____

_____

_____

1. The Problem: _____

2. Possible Solutions: _____

_____

_____

_____

_____

_____

3. What is Good/Bad in Each of the Solutions?: _____

_____

_____

_____

_____

_____

4. The Solution I Will Implement: _____

_____

_____

_____

_____

_____

_____

1. The Problem: _____

2. Possible Solutions: _____

_____

_____

_____

_____

_____

3. What is Good/Bad in Each of the Solutions?: _____

_____

_____

_____

_____

_____

4. The Solution I Will Implement: _____

_____

_____

_____

_____

_____

_____

1. The Problem: _____

2. Possible Solutions: _____

_____

_____

_____

_____

_____

3. What is Good/Bad in Each of the Solutions?: _____

_____

_____

_____

_____

_____

4. The Solution I Will Implement: _____

_____

_____

_____

_____

_____

SOLVING COMMON PROBLEMS

Practice makes it perfect. Instead of pulling yourself down into the vortex of negative behavior, realize there are many ways to train your brain. One of those ways is to keep posing small challenges for yourself every day. These challenges do not have to be ones of the past or ones you have to make up. But rather, these could be challenges you can find anywhere you turn.

What do I mean by this? Well, more than mere puzzles, of course! Solving common problems such as puzzles or brain teasers can help you challenge your mind. But the real thing to incorporate here is a small scheme that can help you get out of your negative thought pattern every time. If you are unsure that you are thinking "out of the box" to the widest extent, then these teasers can help you out.

Here are a few common issues that every teenager faces:

1. A face filled with spots or pimples.
2. Feeling left out in social situations.
3. Feeling overwhelmed with school.
4. Not wanting to do homework every day.
5. Having very low self-esteem and a bad body image.
6. Difficulty connecting with friends.
7. Difficult connecting with siblings and/or parents.
8. Struggling at school.
9. Struggling to fit in in social situations.
10. Feeling unmotivated.
11. Not knowing what to do with yourself and your future.
12. Frequently arguing, with everyone.

Now, let's elaborate on one of these in this exercise. Let's go with number 3 - feeling overwhelmed with school.

The first step you're going to take is to identify the issue - which we have.

The second step is thinking about possible solutions. In this case, you can try to limit your distractions or ask for help.

The third step is to evaluate the solutions. For example, if you ask for help, you may learn more, and become better (one of the pros), but you may feel like you are losing your independence (one of the cons). Limiting your distractions seems like a pretty good idea so far.

The fourth step is to choose the best solution - which is in this case limiting the distractions.

The fifth and final step is to implement the solution. Always start small but do this every day. Start with 10 minutes or half an hour a day and work your way up - as long as you feel good and are comfortable with the process.

Now, go ahead and do some practice yourself.

1. The Problem: _____

2. Possible Solutions: _____

    _____

    _____

    _____

    _____

    _____

3. What is Good/Bad in Each of the Solutions?: _____

    _____

    _____

    _____

    _____

    _____

4. The Solution I Will Implement: _____

    _____

    _____

    _____

    _____

    _____

    _____

1. The Problem: _____

2. Possible Solutions: _____

_____

_____

_____

_____

_____

3. What is Good/Bad in Each of the Solutions?: _____

_____ _____

_____ __ ___

_____

_____

_____

4. The Solution I Will Implement: _____

_____

_____

_____

_____

_____

_____

1. The Problem: _____

2. Possible Solutions: _____

_____

_____

_____

_____

_____

3. What is Good/Bad in Each of the Solutions?: _____

_____

_____

_____

_____

_____

4. The Solution I Will Implement: _____

_____

_____

_____

_____

_____

_____

1. The Problem: _____

2. Possible Solutions: _____

_____

_____

_____

_____

_____

3. What is Good/Bad in Each of the Solutions?: _____

_____

_____

_____

_____

_____

4. The Solution I Will Implement: _____

_____

_____

_____

_____

_____

1. The Problem: _____

2. Possible Solutions: _____

   _____

   _____

   _____

   _____

   _____

3. What is Good/Bad in Each of the Solutions?: _____

   _____

   _____

   _____

   _____

   _____

4. The Solution I Will Implement: _____

   _____

   _____

   _____

   _____

   _____

   _____

1. The Problem: _____

2. Possible Solutions: _____

_____

_____

_____

_____

_____

3. What is Good/Bad in Each of the Solutions?: _____

_____

_____

_____

_____

_____

4. The Solution I Will Implement: _____

_____

_____

_____

_____

_____

1. The Problem: _____

2. Possible Solutions: _____

_____

_____

_____

_____

3. What is Good/Bad in Each of the Solutions?: _____

_____

_____

_____

_____

_____

4. The Solution I Will Implement: _____

_____

_____

_____

_____

_____

1. The Problem: _____

2. Possible Solutions: _____

_____

_____

_____

_____

_____

3. What is Good/Bad in Each of the Solutions?: _____

_____

_____

_____

_____

_____

4. The Solution I Will Implement: _____

_____

_____

_____

_____

_____

1. The Problem: _____

2. Possible Solutions: _____

_____

_____

_____

_____

_____

3. What is Good/Bad in Each of the Solutions?: _____

_____

_____

_____

_____

_____

4. The Solution I Will Implement: _____

_____

_____

_____

_____

_____

_____

1. The Problem: _____

2. Possible Solutions: _____

_____

_____

_____

_____

_____

3. What is Good/Bad in Each of the Solutions?: _____

_____

_____

_____

_____

_____

4. The Solution I Will Implement: _____

_____

_____

_____

_____

_____

1. The Problem: _____

2. Possible Solutions: _____

_____

_____

_____

_____

_____

3. What is Good/Bad in Each of the Solutions?: _____

_____

_____

_____

_____

_____

4. The Solution I Will Implement: _____

_____

_____

_____

_____

_____

_____

1. The Problem: _____

2. Possible Solutions: _____

_____

_____

_____

_____

3. What is Good/Bad in Each of the Solutions?: _____

_____

_____

_____

_____

_____

4. The Solution I Will Implement: _____

_____

_____

_____

_____

_____

_____

Try to do this with every issue you face in life. It is mind-altering how useful these steps can be.

You can still indulge in daily crossword puzzles, sudoku, chess, or anything you find interesting. These games are a fantastic way to enhance your logical thinking. But this exercise is the one thing you need to pull yourself back up. Sure enough, after a while, you will notice yourself thinking outside the box constantly.

SOLUTION IMPLEMENTATION PRACTICE

This last exercise is all about implementing a little bit of everything you've learned so far. The practice of implementing a solution includes understanding the challenge or issue, setting some clear objectives, designing the solution, and allocating the necessary resources to make it happen.

To solve a problem, you need to know how to approach it in a way that would result in a successful resolution. The thing is, as I mentioned earlier, you can't always be sure if what you have in mind as a potential solution would work or not. As the last exercise, this is the simplest one of them all – just try. Give it a go! I know that there may be many things blocking you from making a decision or thinking clearly, but as we are nearing the end of this book, you have to be honest – we did cover almost all of them, right?

So, what I want you to do is to choose one single problem you currently have in your mind. Then go through all the problem-solving steps. Once you have the solution you want to implement, then go and give the solution you have in mind a try. Even if it fails, today's chapter taught you that you can always go back to the brainstorming step and assess the situation from the beginning. Because the solutions you may come up with could be the best ones, but nothing will really happen if you never act on them.

What Did You Learn From This Chapter?

In this chapter, I am hoping to have given you the liberty to think positively with your mind. To challenge yourself every single time and hopefully to have nudged you in the right direction. Without challenges, there is no growth.

Let's make a short recap of what you've learned here:

- ✧ You learned the five steps of problem-solving skills.
- ✧ You had an exercise on how to implement the problem-solving practice.
- ✧ An exercise you need to implement daily – solving common problems.
- ✧ The last exercise that simply nudges you to begin.

So far, this book has been about uplifting you and pushing you forward in life. I can imagine what it must be like for you right now. You finally started believing that you can do anything you set your mind to, and you can create a better and more positive version of yourself. But what will happen if you fall back to your old self? Is there still a voice in the back of your mind telling you that you have a chance of failing, that everything would have been for nothing?

The book's last chapter is about permanently cementing everything you've learned so far. It is about preventing a relapse (should you get to that point). You see – I really did think of everything. I have been where you are and know what you're going through. So, turn the page, and let's take the final steps toward creating a better you – together!

CHAPTER 11

RELAPSE PREVENTION

"Life is very interesting. In the end, some of your greatest pains become your greatest strengths." – Drew Barrymore

With this lovely quote, I open up the book's last chapter. To be honest, Drew Barrymore could not have said it better – turning the pain into your strong side is one of the many joys in life. It is what makes you stronger, more resilient, calmer, more centered, and happier overall.

While all of this is true, word for word, you are still a human and a young one at that. You're still learning. Who knows how many times you're going to fall in life before you lift yourself back up? Each time that happens, you will probably want to get right back into the negative mindset, completely dismissing the CBT approach and everything you've worked so hard for. I understand – you may be faced with extremely challenging situations, which can damage all the progress you've made.

But that doesn't mean you should give up. On the contrary, it means that you should have something to fall back on. I understand where your fear is coming from. Maybe that little voice still tells you that you can never improve, even if you went through this entire book and completed all the exercises with flying colors.

Even if your conscious mind notices the change, your subconscious mind may still make you believe that you are not worthy of anything good. This is known as the turning point in the process, and it is when most people relapse.

Because your progress is important, I decided to dedicate this last chapter to relapse prevention. Let's discuss how to handle yourself in tough times.

Recognizing Warning Signs of Relapse

When you have undergone a program or have used an approach where your sole focus has been yourself, you may feel encouraged once you step out into the world. However, some of you may hesitate about everything because of fear. You may be scared that you will fail and return to your old self. I know that no one wants to have an immediate fear of failure once you step out into the unknown. That is why it is essential to create a relapse prevention plan. It will help you learn how to avoid relapse and will help you gain even more skills on how to handle yourself. Ultimately, it will be the final trick you will have up your sleeve that will keep you in check.

When you've worked so hard to make a better person out of yourself, you walked a long and challenging journey. With each step, you got out of your comfort zone, and you assessed the situation over and over again. The level of self-awareness increased, and everything about you unfolded in stages – right before your eyes. The unfolding part gives you a part of the answer. This is the first thing you need to look into if you have the fear of relapse. The more acute the self-awareness is, the easier it will be to spot any issues.

Ultimately, there are a few signs that can apply to anyone when we talk about relapse. They are:

- ✧ **Emotional relapse** – the denial tends to be strong here. Emotional relapse is the most serious form of relapse here because, after all, we are focusing on thoughts, feelings, and behavior. You may notice feeling isolated and being emotionally reclusive as the first signs. Other than that, you start not being involved in any day-to-day activities, having negative views about yourself and others around you, having difficulty sleeping, and having a reduced concern for personal hygiene.

- ✧ **Mental health** – you start lacking the resistance you worked so hard to obtain. Instead of focusing on the good, taking a step back, and assessing every thought and situation that needs your attention, you stop doing this. You slowly start going back to your old habit of immediately jumping to the wrong and negative conclusions. You notice how the exercises and knowledge you've gained over the past period of time slowly start to slip away from you. Your mental health stops being your priority, and you abide more and more by your past thinking patterns.

Noticing the warning signs of relapse can make you both aware and unaware at the same time. How come? Well, the unaware part is that voice that keeps telling you everything will go wrong, and you're not worth it. The aware part is that you know that you can do better, but you feel like you are constantly pulled under the surface.

Developing a Relapse Prevention Plan

Observing the warning signs I just mentioned is a step in the right direction. To fully prevent yourself from stepping back into your old habits means taking the warning signs seriously. The thoughts that cross your mind don't always need your attention or action. A part of developing a relapse prevention plan means controlling your levels of stress.

Learn to recognize each time when your stress levels go up and are unchecked – especially if you are dealing with anxiety issues. Experiencing anxiety means that you are dismissing the path of dealing with stress healthily.

The main part of your relapse prevention plan should be lowering stress levels. Thankfully, there are a few ways you can naturally achieve this. Here are some examples:

- ✦ Regularly exercising or indulging in physical activity of your liking.
- ✦ Keeping in touch with your friends and family and giving them a little bit of your time.
- ✦ Making a list of feel-good movies and songs that you can turn to every time you feel an onset of negativity creeping up on you.
- ✦ Always focusing on the positive mindset rather than the negative.
- ✦ Maintaining a healthy diet, filled with nutrient-dense foods.
- ✦ Journaling, or any other way of writing down the good things that come to your mind.
- ✦ Celebrating all the milestones you achieve in life, be those small or large.

Since I am ending this list on a celebratory note, I think it is high time to start looking into the strategies, right? The other biggest part of creating a solid relapse prevention plan is creating strong strategies that will help you maintain success. In other words, let's give the spotlight to the bright side of life!

Strategies for Maintaining Progress Over Time

Over time, it is critical to maintain effectiveness and progress. It is not just about reaching a certain point and then remaining there. No. You will develop as a person throughout your life. During this time, you will keep discovering new things about yourself. You will push your limits and strengthen your boundaries. You can't remain in the same spot your entire life – and you won't.

A part of relapse prevention is the list of strategies that can keep you on the right track every single time. And I am talking about much more than open and honest communication with yourself and with others. I am talking about seeing the good, focusing on the good, and achieving the good.

The trick is to keep yourself motivated. Why are you doing all of this? To create a better version of yourself. Do you want to keep working on this? Yes. Why? Because it makes you feel better and achieve more. Do you need to feel pressured about it? Absolutely not!

Find something that will truly motivate you. At this point, I can give you a little nudge in the right direction. Below, you will find a list of a few techniques or strategies that I have learned about along the way that have helped me remain on track. In order to keep on going, try implementing at least a few of them. That way, you'll know you will have done everything for yourself.

All of these are very easy to do. See for yourself below!

1. **A reward** – reward yourself for all the times you have overcome a certain challenge. As you work on yourself and your goals, you will constantly step out of your comfort zone. You will face an increasing number of challenges and give much effort to overcome them. As that happens, reward yourself each time you make it through. Whether it is a milestone you've set for yourself or the consistency you've maintained, never forget to treat yourself.

2. **Relax** – in all fairness, you can't constantly work on yourself. Everybody needs some time to relax, and you are no exception. You may have just gone through an emotional rollercoaster – that means you did quite a demanding job keeping yourself up! So, when you notice that a calmer period is coming, or you just feel like you need to recharge, give yourself that time. This type of recharging can be anything – from drawing yourself a bath to enjoying a hot beverage – anything that can relax you.

3. **Prepare for the day** – the best way to tackle things is not only one at a time but also one day beforehand. By creating a list of the things you need to do the following day, you can have a clear picture of your responsibilities and divide them into smaller sections. By doing this, you can overcome them very easily. Once you know success is guaranteed, nothing is stopping you!

4. **Be realistic and own yourself** – as I mentioned in the SMART goal frame, your goals should always be realistic. You need to be honest with yourself about how much time you would need to achieve or complete something. What I didn't mention is that you should always own your goals. Do whatever you want to carry out because something might constantly push you back or tell you not to do anything. Take responsibility for your actions and carry them out to the very end – you will be glad you did so.

5. **Indulge in a power hour** – when you feel like you have a lot more energy, focus it on something you've been putting on the back burner for a while. This could be any type of tedious task or something you didn't want to face yet. By putting

things in the front line while you have energy, you take advantage of the perfect situation. Instead of doing nothing and then beating yourself up because you've done nothing at the time when you felt you could be active, you're doing something productive. This task could be anything – because you'll see that you will feel lighter as soon as you complete it.

These are only a handful of strategies you can implement to lift any remaining weight off your shoulders. They will slowly pave the way for progress. Before I wrap things up, remember this – progress is still progress, no matter how slow you move. And before you know it, time has passed, and you will look back only to see you've come a long way.

What Did You Learn From This Chapter?

As the last chapter of this book, its goal was to complete the circle – and give you the last bits of information you need to help you on your journey to reinventing yourself. Here is what you learned from it:

- ✧ The progress you make is as important as you say it is.
- ✧ Relapse can happen to anyone – there are a few warning signs that point to it.
- ✧ It is your responsibility to stop the relapse from happening by utilizing the relapse prevention plan.
- ✧ Other than prevention, you can always focus on the good – try using the strategies for maintaining progress over time.

I can only hope that the biggest thing you learned from this chapter is not to beat yourself up every time. Life will happen to you, whether you want it to or not, and you will not be prepared for what it gives you most of the time. However, you must remember how strong you are through all the challenges and especially, the curveballs. You can achieve anything you set your mind to and easily become the best version of yourself. There is no need to fear what's yet to come because whatever it is, through the power of this book, you can overcome it.

CONCLUSION

With this wonderful quote in mind, I would like to bid you one final adieu. As we reach the end of our journey together, I want to reflect on everything we've learned. Now, I am not going to do the regular "let's review what we've learned" since we did that at the end of each chapter. No. I will help you reflect on these lessons, as they will be the most valuable life lessons you will ever learn.

Through this book, you realized there is a way for you to shape your future and yourself, and you learned about all the different strategies you can implement to make that happen. Together, we highlighted the importance of self-control and accentuated your potential for continuous personal development. What you learned here is more than just another skill set. It is the cornerstone of creating a successful, fulfilling, and happy life. Once you realize that you have no trouble mastering self-control and that the CBT approach is the most successful one, you will have gained complete power over your life.

Making deliberate choices that align with your goals and values and what you aspire to be is important.

Managing your time is important.

Resisting falling back into your old ways is important.

Pushing through the most challenging times is important.

Self-control and CBT have helped you achieve just that. By utilizing the tools you found in this book, you will commit to life-long learning and self-improvement. I can only imagine the feeling you got while reading this book – that feeling comes from realizing that we are constantly evolving. There was always room for improvement and development. You just had to find a way to do that. At the end of the day, it is all about abiding by a growing mindset and opening yourself up to all life can offer. Through all the steps you made while reading this book, you noticed that they are still significant, no matter how small they are.

Being a teenager is difficult. Being a teenager in the 21st century seems like the biggest challenge – especially when you're the teenager in question. I can understand that. I did understand that. That's why this book was filled with information that was helpful to you. You learned how to create new habits and keep yourself away from a life that was difficult and negative.

Before we part ways, I leave you with this – always surround yourself with people who are good for you. Always try to look on the bright side. Remember that the choices you make today pave the way for the person you will become in the future. Having full control over yourself and constantly learning is not something you achieve once – but rather something you work on every day. You are willing to make a change, and I know you have both the patience and the determination to make that change possible. Cultivate your mind and move forward through life. Carry the lessons from this book with you and allow them to guide you to create and control the life you've always wanted!

THANK YOU

Thank you so much for purchasing my book.

The marketplace is filled with dozens and dozens of other similar books, but you took a chance and chose this one. I hope it was well worth it.

So again, THANK YOU for getting this book and for making it all the way to the end.

Before you go, I wanted to ask you for one small favor.

Could you please consider posting a review for my book on the platform? Posting a review is the best and easiest way to support the work of independent authors like me.

Your feedback will help me to keep writing the kind of books that will help you get the results you want. It would mean a lot to me to hear from you.

Leave a Review on Amazon US →

Leave a Review on Amazon UK →

ABOUT THE AUTHOR

Emily Carter is an author who loves helping teens with their biggest turning point in life, adulting. She grew up in New York and is happily married to her high school sweetheart. She also has two of her own children.

In her free time, Emily is an avid volunteer at a local food bank and enjoys hiking, traveling, and reading books on personal development. With over a decade of experience in the education and parenting field she has seen the difference that good parenting and the right tips can make in a teenager's life. She is now an aspiring writer through which she shares her insights and advice on raising happy, healthy, and resilient children, teens, and young adults.

Emily's own struggles with navigating adulthood and overcoming obstacles inspired her to write. She noticed a gap in education regarding teaching essential life skills to teens and young adults. She decided to write comprehensive guides covering everything from money and time management to job searching and communication skills. Emily hopes her book will empower teens and young adults to live their best lives and reach their full potential.

To find more of her books, visit her Amazon Author page at:

https://www.amazon.com/author/emily-carter

REFERENCES

Ackerman, C. (2017). *21 Mindfulness Exercises & Activities For Adults (+ PDF)*. Positive Psychology. Available at: https://positivepsychology.com/mindfulness-exercises-techniques-activities/#mindfulness-interventions-techniques-worksheets

Ackerman, C. (2017). *Cognitive Distortions: 22 Examples & Worksheets (& PDF)*. Positive Psychology. Available at: https://positivepsychology.com/cognitive-distortions/#common-cognitive-distortions

Apex Recovery. (2023). *Relapse Prevention: Coping Skills And Warning Signs*. Available at: https://apex.rehab/relapse-prevention-coping-skills-warning-signs/

Ayushka. (2023). *The Art Of Non-Judgment: Cultivating Compassion And Empathy*. Medium. Available at: https://medium.com/@ayusingh2506/the-art-of-non-judgment-cultivating-compassion-and-empathy-158f038c6f2a

Behavioral Therapy? Healthline. Available at: https://www.healthline.com/health/abc-model#benefits-and-examples

Better Help. (2024). *Behaviors, Emotions, And Feelings: How They Work Together*. Available at: https://www.betterhelp.com/advice/behavior/behaviors-emotions-and-feelings-how-they-work-together/

Bonfil, A. & Wagage, S. (2020) *A Course in CBT Techniques: A Free Online CBT Workbook*. Available at: https://cogbtherapy.com/introduction-to-cbt

Calm. (2024). *Reframing Negative Thoughts: How To Challenge Negative Thinking*. Available at: https://www.calm.com/blog/reframing-negative-thoughts

Carroll, D. (2019). *The Relationship Between Thoughts, Feelings, And Behaviors*. Debbie Woodall Carroll. Available at: https://debbiewoodallcarroll.com/the-relationship-between-thoughts-feelings-and-behaviors/

Classroom Mental Health. (2024) Helping Students Connect The Dots: Thoughts, Feelings, & Behaviors. Available at: https://classroommentalhealth.org/in-class/thoughts/

Cleveland Clinic. (2024) *Stress: Coping With Life's Stressors*. Available at: https://my.clevelandclinic.org/health/articles/6392-stress-coping-with-lifes-stressors

Counselling Life Coaching. (2024). *Understanding The Cognitive Triad In Cognitive Behavioral Therapy (CBT)*. Available at: https://counselling-lifecoaching.com/understanding-the-cognitive-triad-in-cognitive-behavioral-therapy-cbt/

Darcy, A. (2023). *Balanced Thinking – What Is It, And How Can You Benefit?* Harley Therapy Mental Health Blog. Available at: https://www.harleytherapy.co.uk/counselling/balanced-thinking-benefits.htm

Davis, T. (2021). *Ultimate Positive Thinking Exercises (+ 3 Great Techniques)*. Positive Psychology. Available at: https://positivepsychology.com/positive-thinking-exercises/#techniques

Delaware Psychological Services. (2021). *10 Ways To Practice Positive Self-Talk*. Available at: https://www.delawarepsychologicalservices.com/post/10-ways-to-practice-positive-self-talk

Get Self Help. (2024) *Positive Coping Statements*. Available at: https://www.getselfhelp.co.uk/positive-coping-statements/

Great Expectations. (2024) *Quotes About Problem-Solving*. Available at: https://www.greatexpectations.org/resources/life-principles/problem-solving/quotes-about-problem-solving/

Grouport. (2024) Empowering CBT Techniques Quotes: Words Of Wisdom For Personal Growth And Cognitive Mastery. Grouport Therapy. Available at: https://www.grouporttherapy.com/blog/cbt-quotes

Health Direct. (2022). *Self-Talk*. Available at: https://www.healthdirect.gov.au/self-talk

Hope + Wellness. (2024). *How To Make A Coping Skills Toolbox*. Available at: https://www.hope-wellness.com/blog/how-to-make-a-coping-skills-toolbox

IIENSTITU. (2023). *Mastering Problem Solving: Daily Exercises To Elevate Your Skills.* LinkedIn. Available at: https://www.linkedin.com/pulse/mastering-problem-solving-daily-exercises-elevate-your-skills/

Indeed. (2022). *What Is Assertiveness Training? Definition, Benefits, And Steps*. Available at: https://www.indeed.com/career-advice/career-development/what-is-assertiveness-training

Kara. (2019). *How To Develop And Implement Healthy Coping Skills Into Your Daily Routine.* Hartzell Counseling. Available at: https://hartzellcounseling.com/how-to-develop-and-implement-healthy-coping-skills-into-your-daily-routine/

Kitazawa, E. (2022). *Behavioral Patterns In Psychology: Learn To Accept Yourself.* Shortform. Available at: https://www.shortform.com/blog/behavioral-patterns-psychology/

Loving Roots Project. (2019). *Using Positive Affirmations To Create A Good Mindset*. Available at: https://www.lovingrootsproject.com/allblogposts/using-positive-affirmations-to-create-a-good-mindset

Maini, N. (2023). *5 Simple Steps To Effective Problem Solving.* Synergogy. Available at: https://synergogy.com/5-simple-steps-to-effective-problem-solving/

Mind Tools. (2024) *Smart Goals*. Available at: https://www.mindtools.com/a4wo118/smart-goals

Mindful. (2024) *Getting Started With Mindfulness*. Available at: https://www.mindful.org/meditation/mindfulness-getting-started/

Mitchell, K. (2017). *15 Positive Thinking Exercises & Activities To Transform Your Life.* Thoughts Catalog. Available at: https://thoughtcatalog.com/kathy-mitchell/2017/03/15-positive-thinking-exercises-activities-to-transform-your-life/

My Self Help Habit. (2020). *Ten Tips For Maintaining Progress Towards Your Goals*. Available at: https://www.myselfhelphabit.co.uk/2020/01/24/ten-tips-for-maintaining-progress-towards-your-goals/

Newport Academy. (2022). *CBT For Teens: How Cognitive Behavioral Therapy Works*. Newport Academy. Available at: https://www.newportacademy.com/resources/mental-health/cbt-treatment/

Newport Academy. (2022). *The 5 Types Of Coping Skills For Teens, Plus 10 Healthy Coping Strategies.* Available at: https://www.newportacademy.com/resources/empowering-teens/coping-skills-teens/

NHS. (2024) Reframing Unhelpful Thoughts. Available at: https://www.nhs.uk/every-mind-matters/mental-wellbeing-tips/self-help-cbt-techniques/reframing-unhelpful-thoughts/

Nunez, K. (2020). *What Is The ABC Model In Cognitive*

Pelzer, K. (2023*). Looking Ahead – 100 Quotes On Strength And Resilience To Help Get Us Through Tough Times*. Parade. Available at: https://parade.com/1012592/kelseypelzer/quotes-for-tough-times/

Pietrangelo, A. (2020). *Is Impulsive Behavior A Disorder?* Healthline. Available at: https://www.healthline.com/health/mental-health/impulsive-behavior#causes

Positive Mind Works. (2023). *The Importance Of Assertive Communication*. Available at: https://www.positivemindworks.co/the-importance-of-assertive-communication/

Problem Solving (2024) How Do You Implement Your Solution? LinkedIn. Available at: https://www.linkedin.com/advice/0/how-do-you-implement-your-solution-skills-problem-solving

Raypole, C. (2020). *How To Identify And Manage Your Emotional Triggers.* Healthline. Available at: https://www.healthline.com/health/mental-health/emotional-triggers#finding-yours

Raypole, C. (2022). *How To Do A Body Scan Meditation (And Why You Should)*. Healthline. Available at: https://www.healthline.com/health/body-scan-meditation#how-to-do-it

Rice, A. (2021). *How To Challenge Negative Self-Talk*. Psych Central. Available at: https://psychcentral.com/lib/challenging-negative-self-talk

Shawn, B. (2009) *61 Self-Control Quotes That Can Change Your Life.* Happy Publishing. Available at: https://www.happypublishing.com/blog/self-control-quotes/

Sutton, J. (2021). *How To Perform Assertiveness Training: 6 Exercises*. Positive Psychology. Available at: https://positivepsychology.com/assertiveness-training/#assertiveness

Vallejo, M. (2022). *Automatic Negative Thoughts (Ants): How To Identify And Fix Them*. Mental Health Center Kids. Available at: https://mentalhealthcenterkids.com/blogs/articles/automatic-negative-thoughts

Vogel, K. (2022). *The Basic Principles Of Cognitive Behavioral Therapy.* PsychCentral. Available at: https://psychcentral.com/pro/the-basic-principles-of-cognitive-behavior-therapy#basic-principles

WebMD. (2023). *What Is Box Breathing?* Available at: https://www.webmd.com/balance/what-is-box-breathing

Whitworth, E. (2023). *8 Radical Acceptance Exercises To Help You Be Fully Present*. Shortform. Available at: https://www.shortform.com/blog/radical-acceptance-exercises/

Made in United States
North Haven, CT
28 April 2025

68401006R00091